BRAIN GAMES

for

WORD NERDS

Francis Heaney

PUZZLE
WRIGHT
PRESS

New York

PUZZLE
WRIGHT
PRESS
New York

An Imprint of Sterling Publishing
1166 Avenue of the Americas
New York, NY 10036

PUZZLEWRIGHT PRESS and the distinctive Puzzlewright Press logo are registered
trademarks of Sterling Publishing Co., Inc.

© 2011 by Francis Heaney

ISBN 978-1-4027-7095-1 (paperback)

Distributed in Canada by Sterling Publishing
ℂ⁄ₒ Canadian Manda Group, 664 Annette Street
Toronto, Ontario, Canada M6S 2C8
Distributed in the United Kingdom by GMC Distribution Services
Castle Place, 166 High Street, Lewes, East Sussex, England BN7 1XU
Distributed in Australia by Capricorn Link (Australia) Pty. Ltd.
P.O. Box 704, Windsor, NSW 2756, Australia

For information about custom editions, special sales, and premium and
corporate purchases, please contact Sterling Special Sales at 800-805-5489 or
specialsales@sterlingpublishing.com.

Manufactured in the United States of America

4   6   8   10   9   7   5   3

CONTENTS

INTRODUCTION

There's an event I have attended every year since 1995: the National Puzzlers' League convention, which is so densely packed with wordplay lovers that it is always on the verge of collapsing into a logological black hole from which no anagram can escape.

The convention is held in a different city every year, and although many things have changed in that time, one thing has tended to remain constant: Each of those cities will write an article about us in its local newspaper, and each of those articles will invariably refer to the members of the National Puzzlers' League as "word nerds."

"Word nerds." It always felt like a condescending turn of phrase, and we would roll our eyes each time we saw it. But who can blame the reporters for resorting to it so often? It rhymes, it's catchy, and maybe ... just *maybe* ... it's true. We are, after all, a group that, every summer, sits indoors in a hotel on beautiful sunny days and solves word puzzles. Is there really something else to call us?

Personally, though, I've always felt that being a nerd was the best possible life choice. And popular culture has been catching up to this viewpoint, so I think it's time to let our geek flag fly and reclaim our identity: Say it loud! We're word nerds and we're proud!

As you'll see in this book, my taste in word puzzles is rather eclectic; I like a lot of variety from one puzzle to the next. Some puzzles are what you might call "pure wordplay": taking words and playing with their letters without being particularly concerned about the individual meanings of the words. Others involve crossword-style clues, trivia, quotations, grids, and even a little bit of arithmetic. Many are based on familiar types of wordplay—anagrams, letter changes, and such—but have had extra twists added along the way. And some puzzles, it turned out, were too much fun to stop writing, and so they recur throughout the book. If you decide you enjoy any of those puzzles enough that you simply have to skip ahead, here's where to find them: Blanking Out (pages 7, 28, 39, 53, 81); Jigsaw Squares (12, 19, 34, 66, 92); Internal Affairs (13, 44, 73, 97); Mixed Messages (15, 25, 57, 76); Misdirection (22, 60, 84); Entertainment Options (36, 68); and Dropquote/Floatquote (38, 64, 89).

Anyway, now that I've finished writing this book, I will return to my regular life. Of course, my regular life consists of a lot of moments where I spontaneously notice that if you change both long "e" sounds in WHEELIE to long "a" sounds, you get WAYLAY; or that if you take the name of the GYRO KING restaurant down the street from my apartment and replace the word OK with the word AT, you get the word GYRATING ... so perhaps it won't be that much of a change for me. But such is the curse—and the consolation—of the word nerd.

(For more information about the National Puzzlers' League, visit http://www.puzzlers.org.)

—Francis Heaney

BLANKING OUT

In the lists of words and phrases below, some letters have
been replaced with blanks. Fill in those blanks with sets of
thematically related words to restore the lists. For instance, given
_ M _ _ P _ T E _ T and _ T _ N D A R D   _ _ _ _ _ _, you
would write in ONION and SAUSAGE (both pizza toppings) to
make OMNIPOTENT and STANDARD USAGE.

1.
_ O _ R _ _ I _ G
S _ L L _ B _ _
_ _ _ _ T A G O _
_ _ O V _ _ _ _ _ _ W _

Theme: _____

2.
_ I _ M _ _ _ N T
_ _ _ _ _ P P O _ _ R
_ _ _ _ E G _ D L _
_ H O _ _ _ _ F _ E R
_ O _ H I _ L O _ _ N

Theme: _____

3.
_ _ S H I O _ I S _ _
D Y S _ _ _ _ _ _ A
_ O U T _ E _ _ _ _ A S I _
_ E M I _ _ _ _ V A _ _
_ I _ E _ _ _ _ _ P E
_ A _ R D _ _ S _ E R
C I _ _ P _ _ L E
_ _ _ _ O _ U E N E _ S

Theme: _____

4.
A P _ _ _ _ I Z _ _ _
_ _ T _ I _ _ D _ L
A D _ _ _ C E _ T
_ _ U _ L I N _
A _ S _ R _ A _ I L I T _
E L E _ T _ O _ _ A _

Theme: _____

5.
_ _ _ C R A _ _
G R _ _ _ D _ _ _ _ C E
_ _ _ _ A L Y _ T
_ I N _ _ _ Y _ _ _ _ B E R
_ _ R B O _ _ _ _ O X I _ _
_ _ _ L A _ I N _
_ _ _ _ I O N
_ _ R E E _
C _ _ N _ _ _ _ I N G
L O _ _ _ N _ _ _
_ _ _ _ _ L _ C E _ C _
L _ _ _ _ A _ H _ N
C I _ A _ _ _ T T E C _ _ _ _
_ _ _ _ _ _ D _ A B
P _ _ _ G _ A N _

Theme: _____

OVERLAP OF LUXURY

The clues in this puzzle all lead to two-word phrases; for instance, the clue "Speedy move executed by someone mixing cocoa" leads to the phrase FAST STIR. All the answer phrases can have their first and second words overlapped by at least two letters, and deleting the overlapping letters results in a new word formed from the leftovers. (For instance, deleting the overlapping ST in FAST STIR gives the word FAIR.) The clues and the leftover words are given separately. Your job is to match them and supply the missing two-word phrases.

CLUES

_____ 1. Advertisement you just can't look away from

_____ 2. Prescription used to keep spouses from getting chronically distracted

_____ 3. Chewy candy reacts to being heated up

_____ 4. Location of ink cartridges, perhaps

_____ 5. What you need if you want to enter the top secret areas of a reactor

_____ 6. Temperature control that's lowest on the wall

_____ 7. Delete poetry

_____ 8. Oxidized look that all the cool people are wearing

_____ 9. Proceed in the bee after being given a synonym of "BB"

_____ 10. Panicked reaction from an unscrupulous lawyer

_____ 11. Depressing news about the place where the sheep graze

_____ 12. Give the proper due to something you need to make jelly

_____ 13. Ill-considered thing to be teaching someone

_____	**14.**	The strong airflow that had been slowing down the plane let up somewhat
_____	**15.**	Whiskey holder not quite placed correctly
_____	**16.**	Teens that live in a marshy part of Louisiana
_____	**17.**	Nap that requires the most cleaning up afterward
_____	**18.**	Shiny jewelry worn in an Irish metropolis
_____	**19.**	Mogul of the African shirt industry
_____	**20.**	Terriers in twos
_____	**21.**	Red bird that's the new logo for a rum company
_____	**22.**	Mixture that won't suddenly explode
_____	**23.**	Sleeveless top covered with deadly poison
_____	**24.**	Lone fireplace alcove
_____	**25.**	Handy shortcut for reading Sanskrit religious texts
_____	**26.**	Make the coroner's workplace less vulnerable to bombs and such
_____	**27.**	Select whose paintings to display in the art studio

---

LEFTOVER WORDS

ARGUE	HYPE	RECKON
BANAL	LETTER	REMORSE
BATH	MAIN	RESIN
CARATS	MEANER	RULE
CURLIER	MESA	SET
DASHING	NEAT	SICS
DUG	NUANCE	SNOOK
FLEW	PALES	STAND
HEALED	PRIOR	TANK

Answer, page 100   9

UNDERGROUND FILM FESTIVAL

This film festival is so secret, the list of movies being shown is never openly revealed. Instead, the schedule is concealed in a list of sentences, each containing two hidden items: a movie title and the last name of one of that movie's stars. For instance, the sentence "You probably knew I was nerdy" contains the movie title *Up* (in "yoU Probably") and its star, (Ed) Asner (in "wAS NERdy"). Either the title or star may come first, and the movie title or surname may be more than one word. How many can you find?

1. Tipsy chorus girls smile seductively.
2. My Jungian therapist made a new diagnosis.
3. If you're smart, you can avoid being assimilated by the Borg, nine times out of ten.
4. He plays maracas in order to conceal his tone-deafness.
5. A drumbeat typically makes me wish Tarzan were here.
6. The patient with ulcers and nausea made use of the pharmacy.
7. Hazel ignored the small Englishman.
8. A psychic, a golfer, and Roger Ebert walked into a bar.
9. Clothes tinged with hot pink are geared for dancers.
10. At rehearsal, Dan always wears a cravat around his neck.
11. Don't panic rashly or run around like a frantic headless chicken.
12. A lot of Argonauts escaped from a cyclops.
13. Shop at Tony's for men's cotton shirts.
14. In concert, Raffi can yodel to roomfuls of children.
15. "I enjoy watching NASCAR only when I'm drinking," I giggle.
16. Being an extrovert, I go to all the bars a casanova knows about.
17. Are the benefits of shiatsu permanent, or will I need more eventually?
18. I'm ashamed to tell you why the rathskeller management threw me out.

19. Salad, dinner, and dessert will, I am sorry to report, be delayed.
20. "Right this way—Zelda is a charming hostess, you'll find."
21. My banjo lies unused now that I'm in this alt-rock band.
22. In Cairo, both of us suffered from ostracism, I think.
23. A ballad doesn't punish an eardrum like heavy metal.
24. Wasn't it a nice plan to make watching something comedic a priority?
25. I should start reknitting the sweater for that mannequin today.
26. At a picnic, a bare torso isn't unseemly or kinky.
27. Stop hating show tunes and become pro-Gershwin.
28. Of the muscatel, cider, and mead, the wine is the smoothest one.
29. In denial, I enter the store to which I owe a very large debt.
30. When a hymn is boring, Lutherans omit the chorus sometimes.
31. More drivers on the highway need lessons.
32. With untrained gardeners, don't request wisteria bushes.
33. How toxic are "llama nuggets," Martha?
34. Having a gazpacho meal on Easter night isn't traditional.
35. Attila, with frenzied anger, ousted a Visigoth.
36. I'll never hire an actor till a flattering remark is spoken to me ... is that extra-cynical?
37. Kellogg ran the niftiest cereal company—he's such a rad entrepreneur!
38. This essay on arachnophobia keeps quoting *Charlotte's Web* randomly.
39. An iceberg mangled the ship as it was making a slight course correction.
40. After renting her a grass hut, Teri's landlord acted gruff, aloof, and snippy.

Answer, page 100

JIGSAW SQUARES

In this puzzle, multiple word squares are linked together, forming new words where they connect. For instance, if the top row of the left-hand grid read BRAN, and the bottom row of the top grid read DISH, they would link up to make BRANDISH. Each square's clues are listed separately, with Across and Down clues separated but otherwise in no particular order. Use the long words (also clued separately) to determine which square goes where.

NEW WORDS
- Tart-tasting
- Breathing heavily
- ___ the wheel
- Member of an old Jewish sect

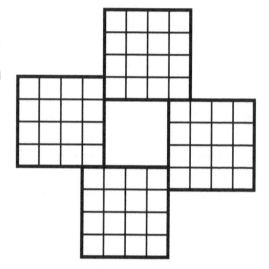

SQUARE 1

Across
- Nefarious
- Christmas decor
- Tarzan transport
- French refusals

Down
- Small square?
- Old matinee idol Novello
- Let off steam
- "If all ___ fails ..."

SQUARE 2

Across
- *Pygmalion* playwright
- "Gotcha": 2 wds.
- Lion feature
- Per

Down
- Roller coaster cry
- Actor Lukas
- Retin-A target
- Conductor's start?

SQUARE 3

Across
- Observed
- Famed race horse ___ Lap
- Jiffy ___ (car care chain)
- Trademarked tangelo

Down
- Enormous
- Bridle attachment
- Asset
- Up to the task

SQUARE 4

Across
- Shoots with a laser gun
- Ex-senator Hart
- Brand of squishy toy balls
- "Egads!": 2 wds.

Down
- *Eureka* network
- On the briny
- "Gotcha," after an insult
- Henry VIII's last wife

Answer, page 102

INTERNAL AFFAIRS

For each of the following pairs of words, one can be inserted inside the other to make a new word—but only after changing one letter in the internal word. For instance, given the pair of words ALE and START, you can change the E in ALE to a W, then insert ALW inside START to make STALWART. (Either word may come first.) When you solve each pair of words, make a note of the new letter; those new letters, read in sequence for each set of puzzles, will spell another pair of words with the same property as a bonus puzzle. And now, let's get all these affairs in order.

1. BLITZ ORATE   _____   ___
   LISTEN NONET   _____   ___
   TINE URGENT   _____   ___
   DIED SCORN   _____   ___
   LUNG SPED   _____   ___
   CHEAT PLANE   _____   ___
   DOE GHOUL   _____   ___
   FORTE MULE   _____   ___
   DEED POLISH   _____   ___
   DIARY SPANS   _____   ___
   AMOUR PART   _____   ___
   Bonus: _____

2. CHICK OUST   _____   ___
   PUNCH SEER   _____   ___
   BLUNT VARY   _____   ___
   PLAID STEER   _____   ___
   CONNORS TRADE   _____   ___
   HARD OMEN   _____   ___
   PUP UNCLE   _____   ___
   Bonus: _____

PRODUCT REPLACEMENT

Product placement has become a very prominent feature of movies, but not until now has it become a feature of everyday language. A number of companies have gone so far as to pay certain words to kick out a competing brand and replace it with their own (ignoring punctuation, if any). For instance, TOM'S toothpaste might replace the CREST in CRESTFALLEN to make TOMSFALLEN. Can you see through the adspeak to find the original words?

1. FLORNADOONERDAIN _____
2. DISTEMPURPEDICTION _____
3. ULTIMAROLAIDS _____
4. INCHIQUITANT _____
5. FORDENCE _____
6. ASPAPREGOS _____
7. SUCHEVRONAR _____
8. DAQUAFINACE _____
9. HITIDERCHY _____
10. EXSTRIDEANT _____
11. CLOTSTARZUND _____
12. ASUAVEURE _____
13. MECERTS _____
14. VIBEACH _____
15. MELIPTONIC _____
16. LEVERECT _____
17. BORIBMO _____
18. ATALAMOM _____
19. DEPRADANG _____
20. OCOMEGAN _____
21. HARASKER _____
22. GOCESARSTS _____
23. BAGEROLE _____
24. MALIFEES _____
25. PIAJAXER _____
26. TEDIESELE _____
27. MOPUMAR _____
28. TWISE _____
29. SOST _____
30. BASSOON _____

Answer, page 102

MIXED MESSAGES

In these puzzles, short quotations have been respaced and anagrammed to make lists of words. For instance, the words in the list SEA DIARIES HADN'T ENO can be anagrammed, respectively, to EAS, IERSAID, THAND, and ONE—which, when respaced, becomes "Easier said than done." The enumerations of the quotations are given beneath the blanks, which are followed by the speaker of the quotation.

1. REINVENT PURER MOONSET GIDEON HAW TOY SAUDI CLOUD BONNETED

____ _____ _____ ____ ___
 5   9   7   5   4

___ ____ _____ __ ____. — Amelia Earhart
 3   4   6'1   2   4

2. LACE INSOBRIETY HEW OINKS TOWN MOAN OSPREY SHINGLES HEDDA TOKENS OWN

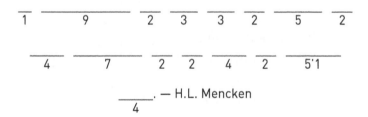

_ _____ __ __ __ __ ____ __
1   9   2 3 3 2   5   2

____ _____ __ __ ___ __ _____
 4   7   2 2   4   2   5'1

____. — H.L. Mencken
 4

3. THIEF SQUIRTER MERE FONT SAT A-TEAMS HINTS BULLETHEAD

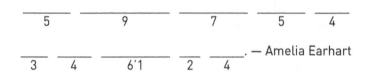

___ _____ _____ __ _ _____
 3   5   11   2 1   9

__ ____ __ __ ____. — Dean Acheson
 2   4   2 2   4

RHYME TIME

I was wondering one day (because I'm the sort of person who wonders these things) how easy it would be to recognize common sayings if every word were replaced with a rhyming word. Not too hard, it turns out. But what if you alphabetize the new words? Now that's actually kind of tricky. For instance, the saying "Penny wise, pound foolish" could be represented by the words ANY GHOULISH ROUND PIES. Phrases are ordered not necessarily by difficulty, but by their total number of words.

1. CHALK CREEP FIZZ   _____
2. GONE SLIME STARCHES   _____
3. CHASED RACED SNAKES   _____
4. HONKERS SHOVE SMALL   _____
5. COLLEGE FLOWER QUIZ   _____
6. JUNCTION STORM SWALLOWS   _____
7. JUICE PINK STRIPS ZIPS   _____
8. CHUNKY FLUNKY TEA VIEW   _____
9. BUN FLAIR FLAT GRIN   _____
10. BRITAIN DUNCE HIGH NICE   _____
11. CACTUS CREW CUT SPEECH   _____
12. EVER FRIGHTENING MICE TYKES   _____
13. BET BREAK FLEET STEM   _____
14. FLOW PLAN QUEST STRUNG   _____
15. BOGS KEEPING WET WHY   _____
16. CHEESY SLEAZY THROW YUM   _____
17. BUBBLES PLEASE THUMB WIN   _____
18. BRUISERS GREGOR'S PLANT WHEE   _____
19. DAUGHTERS LEAP QUILL SPUN   _____
20. BANDS FORM SMART STROLLED   _____
21. AIRS CHASE FOAM PSYCH WHOA   _____
22. HATES MIME MORE SHOW SPAN   _____

23. DUTY KEEP LONELY PIN WHIZ _____

24. ACHE JENNY QUITE SMIRK STANDS _____

25. BED MAILS SMELL THOUGH WHEN _____

26. CARES CHOIR CROAK HEIR PAIRS _____

27. DEVIL OTTER PIQUES SPLITS TONE _____

28. BORROW EAT LIZ TOUCH STARTING

_____

29. ANT BRIGHT PRETTY SMALL THREW

_____

30. DOUBT POUR SCHNOOK SLUMBER SUN

_____

31. FLAKE LABORS SHOULD TENSES WOOD

_____

32. BIRDS CAN CHOWDER FRACTIONS WEEK

_____

33. CALVING CLIMB DEN ONE PRIZE SURE

_____

34. CRITTERS HAT HIS SHOT SMALL STROLLED

_____

35. ART LADEN NUN QUAINT SEVER WHERE

_____

36. AID FEE FOOLS HER NEW OAKEN

_____

37. CUP DUMB FROWN POSE SHUT THRUST

_____

38. FLU GREW PLATE PLUM SHOULD SHOWS WINGS

_____

39. BALD BAR CUT FROZEN HUE LENNY STAR

_____

40. BATCH BLUE FLY PLAQUE STYLE THATCH TOURS

_____

FLIPPERS

These words can be linked to make new words; however, one word must first be reversed. For instance, the words NET and DON could make TENDON (after flipping the word NET). The left-hand word will always precede the right-hand word, but either half may flip (so TEN and NOD could also make TENDON). Can you link them all?

1.	APES	_____	**a.**	AGE
2.	ARC	_____	**b.**	AIL
3.	ARE	_____	**c.**	AN
4.	AREA	_____	**d.**	ARE
5.	ASH	_____	**e.**	CITE
6.	BAN	_____	**f.**	CLING
7.	BAR	_____	**g.**	DELL
8.	BRAG	_____	**h.**	DRAT
9.	BUS	_____	**i.**	DUE
10.	CARTER	_____	**j.**	EGAD
11.	CURT	_____	**k.**	ELK
12.	DUO	_____	**l.**	HELL
13.	ELF	_____	**m.**	HIM
14.	FLAM	_____	**n.**	HOT
15.	FLEW	_____	**o.**	KING
16.	FOLD	_____	**p.**	LANED
17.	GAME	_____	**q.**	LED
18.	GANG	_____	**r.**	LORE
19.	HEAR	_____	**s.**	MAR
20.	KIN	_____	**t.**	NAMES
21.	LAP	_____	**u.**	NET
22.	LEO	_____	**v.**	NIKE
23.	NAMES	_____	**w.**	ONE
24.	NOR	_____	**x.**	RATE
25.	PAR	_____	**y.**	SCALLION
26.	PARES	_____	**z.**	SET
27.	RAM	_____	**aa.**	SHED
28.	SKI	_____	**bb.**	SHY
29.	STOP	_____	**cc.**	SPACE
30.	STUN	_____	**dd.**	STENO
31.	SUM	_____	**ee.**	SURE
32.	TIMES	_____	**ff.**	TABLE
33.	TRAPS	_____	**gg.**	TICS
34.	TWIN	_____	**hh.**	TOR
35.	WARD	_____	**ii.**	TRY
36.	WHIT	_____	**jj.**	UNCTION

Answer, page 103

JIGSAW SQUARES 2

See page 12 for instructions.

NEW WORDS
- Edward Lear verse, often
- A real bundle of nerves?
- Major's predecessor
- Egregious

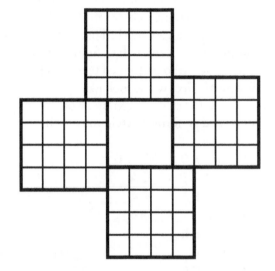

SQUARE 1
Across
- Volcano's output
- The Sharks or the Jets, e.g.
- Worry
- "You said it!"

Down
- Drink created by the inventor of Pop Rocks
- Hindu deity
- Divisible by 2
- Man-made object on the moon

SQUARE 2
Across
- *Burlesque* star
- Hooey
- He was Obi-Wan
- Fashion designer Gernreich

Down
- Option for online TV-watching
- Ill-tempered one
- "We'll always have Paris" speaker
- Temptation site

SQUARE 3
Across
- Half-human, half-goat beast
- ___ *Championship Season* (Pulitzer Prize–winning play revived on Broadway in 2011)
- Lift on the slopes: Hyph.
- Tiny organism in a lake

Down
- Out-of-control tirade
- ___-Hartley Act
- Water, in Juárez
- As boring as can be

SQUARE 4
Across
- *Lambert the Sheepish* ___ (classic Disney cartoon)
- Cheese with a red rind
- ___ facto
- Jay who hosted *Last Comic Standing*

Down
- Shuffle or Nano, e.g.
- Cliff's neighbor at the bar, on *Cheers*
- Gimlet flavoring
- Workplace watchdog: Abbr.

Answer, page 104

TOO MANY NOTES

The musical scale consists of the notes A through G. So what do these fancy modern songwriters think they're doing, using H's and Z's and everything in between? We like things the old-fashioned way, thank you very much. That's why we've deleted everything but the letters A through G from these song titles (and from the musical acts who performed them), so Janis Joplin's "Me and Bobby McGee" would look like __ E A __ __ B __ B B __ __ C G E E. See if you can figure out our playlist, and match up the songs and performers while you're at it.

1. B __ A C __   D __ G
2. __ A B A __ B A
3. G __ E A __   B A __ __ __   __ F F __ __ E
4. B E __ __ E __ E
5. C __ E E __
6. B E A __ __   __ F B __ __ D E __
7. E __ E A __ __ __   __ __ G B __
8. __ A __ __ A C __ A __ E __ E __ __
9. B __ E B __ E   __ __ __ E
10. __ __ A __ D B __   __ E
11. B A __ __ E __   C A __ E
12. __ A __ __ B E __ __ __   B E __ E __
13. C __ A __ __   __ F F __ __ __ __ __
14. __ A __ B E __ __ E __ E
15. D __ E A __ __
16. G __ __ D   __ __ B __ A __ __ __ __ __ __
17. __ __ __ __ E __   C A __ __ F __ __ __ __ __ A
18. F A __ __ __ __
19. C __ A __ G E __
20. G E __ __ E   __ __ A B __ __ __ __ __ E
21. __ A __ __ A B E
22. __ E A __ __   __ __   __ E A __ E __
23. C A __ __   __ E
24. __ A B __ __ A G E

20

25. _ _ G _ E
26. _ _ B _ E _ _ A _ E A _   _ _ _ _ E _ _ _ C _
    B _ _ E _
27. C _ _ _ F _ _ _ _ A B _ _ _   _ _ _ B
28. E _ _ _ E _   _ A _ _ D _ A _
29. _ E A _ _ _ B _ E A _ E _
30. _ A D _   _ A _ _ _ A _ A D E
31. _ _ _ C E   _ _   A   _ _ _ F E _ _ _ _ E
32. B _ _ _ E _ _ _ A _   _ _ _ A _ _ _ _ D _
33. _ A _ A _ A
34. _ A _ E _ F A _ _ _ _

a. C _ _ _ C _ _   B E _ _ _ _
b. _ _ _ E   E A G _ E _
c. D A _ _ _ D   B _ _ _ _ E
d. _ A D _ _ _ _ E A D
e. G _ E E _   D A _
f. C _ _ _ _ _ _ E
   C _ _ _ B
g. E _ _ _ C
   C _ A _ _ _ _ _
h. _ _ _ E   B E A C _
   B _ _ _ _
i. B _ _ _ _ _ D _ E
j. F _ E E _ _ _ _ _ D
   _ A C
k. G E _ _ _ G E
   _ _ _ C _ A E _
l. _ E _ _ _ _   _ E E
   _ E _ _ _ _
m. _ _ _ E   B E A _ _ _ E _
n. B _ B   D _ _ _ A _
o. C _ E _ _
p. B E _   E.   _ _ _ _ G
q. _ A _   B E _ A _ A _
r. _ A D _ _ _ _ A

s. _ E _ A _ _ _ _ C A
t. C _ _ _ _ _ _ _ _ _ A
   A G _ _ _ _ E _ A
u. _ A _ _ _ _ _ G
   _ E A D _
v. B E A _ _ _ _ E
   B _ _ _ _
w. _ E D
   _ E _ _ E _ _ _ _
x. _ _ E   _ _ _ _ _ _ _ G
   _ _ _ _ E _
y. _ _ _ E E _
z. _ _ _ _ _   F _ _ _ _ D
aa. _ _ _ _ _ C E
bb. _ A _   _ A _ E _
cc. _ _ E   E _ _ E _ _ _ _
    B _ _ _ _ _ _ E _ _
dd. _ _ _ C
ee. _ _ _ _ C E   G _ _ _ _ _
ff. A _ E _ _ _ A
    F _ A _ _ _ _ _ _
gg. _ A B E _ _ _ E
hh. _ _ _ _ C _ _ _ E
    _ A _ E _ _ _

Answer, page 104

MISDIRECTION

In this skeleton-style crossword, answers may be entered normally or backward. However, it seemed unfair not to indicate in some way which entries were reversed, so the clues for those entries have all been reversed as well—but definitionwise instead of letterwise. That is to say, they clue the opposites of their corresponding grid entries ... although "opposite" is often interpreted rather loosely, often indicating an opposing counterpart of a different sort than just GOOD vs. BAD. For instance, if the word LAUREL appeared reversed in the grid as LERUAL, it might be clued as "Hale and healthy" (a clue for Laurel's counterpart, HARDY), whereas YDRAH might be clued as "Plant in a winner's wreath" (a clue for Hardy's counterpart, LAUREL). Oh, yes, right, sorry, in case that wasn't clear, while the word being clued is the opposite of the grid entry, it might not be clued in the sense in which it's the opposite of the grid entry. Or even pronounced the same, necessarily. Anyway! Exactly half the entries in the puzzle will be reversed, so that's something.

ACROSS

1   Name in many court cases
3   Prom dress adornments
8   Papal pronouncement
9   Bread, to Brigitte
11 Word repeated in a William Faulkner title
12 William Morris worker, e.g.
13 He sought the Golden Fleece
15 They may say "You are here"
18 "Every Breath You Take" singer
19 Judge played by Paul Newman in 1972: 2 wds.
21 *Brideshead Revisited* author Waugh
22 Discipline featuring downward-facing dogs
23 Vies for the title
24 Philosopher some have theorized was the author of Shakespeare's plays

DOWN

1 Country whose 2006 movie *The Lives of Others* won an Oscar for Best Foreign Language Film

2 Lock of hair

4 Accessway to an expressway: Hyph.

5 Gets in touch with

6 Colossal

7 Ireland's patron, for short: 2 wds.

10 *It Happened One Night* star: 2 wds.

14 Four quarters, in paper form

16 Southwestern capital whose name translates to "holy faith": 2 wds.

17 2001 Jonathan Franzen novel, with *The*

18 Some supermarket workers

20 Crouch to avoid getting hit

Answer, page 104

ODD AND EVEN

In the lists of 8-letter words and phrases below, pairs of entries (one from each list) can be matched up so that, if you read the odd letters of one and the even letters of the other, you'll get a new word (possibly capitalized or hyphenated). For instance, the odd letters of SWATCH plus the even letters of ACCRUE combine to make SCARCE. Odd and even halves may appear on either list.

1.	ARRIVERS	_____	a.	ASSAILED
2.	CALL UPON	_____	b.	BEAT POET
3.	CAVEGIRL	_____	c.	BEDROCKS
4.	DIVERGED	_____	d.	BLITHELY
5.	DRYLANDS	_____	e.	BOATLOAD
6.	FRACTURE	_____	f.	BOX ELDER
7.	FROTHILY	_____	g.	CALMNESS
8.	GLIBNESS	_____	h.	COLTRANE
9.	GOLD MINE	_____	i.	COURTESY
10.	HAZELNUT	_____	j.	CURLED UP
11.	HOMEWARD	_____	k.	CYBERSEX
12.	KEN BURNS	_____	l.	DEMENTED
13.	LIFE MASK	_____	m.	FARTHING
14.	MONOTINT	_____	n.	HELPMATE
15.	MUDPACKS	_____	o.	LAID-BACK
16.	PINPOINT	_____	p.	MISGAUGE
17.	POLICING	_____	q.	MOTORCAR
18.	PUP TENTS	_____	r.	PHARISEE
19.	REARWARD	_____	s.	REDEPLOY
20.	REASCEND	_____	t.	RHAPSODY
21.	STARLING	_____	u.	SEMINARS
22.	SUBSISTS	_____	v.	SIROCCOS
23.	TARRAGON	_____	w.	SNOWBIRD
24.	THEORIZE	_____	x.	TONE POEM
25.	THREATEN	_____	y.	TORTUOUS
26.	TILAPIAS	_____	z.	TRIASSIC
27.	YOGI BEAR	_____	aa.	WORDBOOK

Answer, page 105

MIXED MESSAGES 2

See page 15 for instructions.

1. HEWN VEE FALLER TOWEL BLEMISHES RAP INKSTAIN
WHOSE GINO GOT OVATE STEAMING

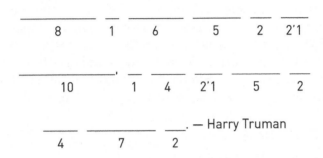

_____ ___ _____ _____ ___ ___
8   1   6   5   2   2'1

_____,' __ _____ ___ _____ ___
10   1 4   2'1 5   2

____ _____ ___. — Harry Truman
4   7   2

2. ITINERANT SALON PRO WAIST WRIT SOUTH OH INGOT

_____ _____ ___ ___
13   5   2   3

_____ _____. — George Orwell
7   8

3. NOME SHUT EVA ARETHA FOOTNOTES TRADE HEED
OATH LIFT LENT BELLY NICKED WITS THOU GAUL
NIGH

___ ___ ___ ___ ___ ___ ___ ___ ___
3   4   4   1   5   2   5   2   4

___ ___ ___ ___ ___ ___ ___
3   5   2   6   4   2   7

_____ _____. — Oscar Wilde
7   8

ON WITH THEIR HEADS

We've taken 50 nine-letter words, broken them into three blocks of three letters, then found three uncapitalized words, each starting with a different one of those blocks. Given those words (alphabetized after deleting the first three letters), your goal is to deduce the word we started with, by restoring the missing letters and correctly arranging the three-letter blocks. So, for instance, the strings ARGOT, LTALE, and RETTA come from the original word TELESCOPE (making the words TELLTALE, ESCARGOT, and OPERETTA). There may be multiple ways to add three letters to the starts of some of the leftover letter strings, but only one choice will let you spell a nine-letter word. Can you crack them all?

1. BUST   NAGE   ZVAH   _____

2. EIGN   HAPS   INGUE   _____

3. HALT   ISAN   THYST   _____

4. FAIT   LISH   SO   _____

5. ARATE   ETTE   IZON   _____

6. OOSE   PAGE   UME   _____

7. CRITY   MINUS   SINET   _____

8. AYIST   DRED   GRANT   _____

9. GNETTE   ICAN   XY   _____

10. PO   SPOOL   TULA   _____

11. AKLY   OMOUS   SURE   _____

12. NIA   TASY   UXE   _____

13. RITO   SENED   STION   _____

14. EGRAL   REMIST   SMA   _____

15. BIL   IKER   MTH   _____

16. ADA   LUNK   UITION   _____

17. MLIN   OLLEE   PAH   _____

18. IOD   RNMENT   TINY   _____

19. FEATER   MISH   PKIN   _____

20. GDOM TREL ZZY _____
21. ABI LURIUM ROGYNY _____
22. ATSU DITY OGANY _____
23. ATOSE DEM GUIN _____
24. ICON LIGAN SILY _____
25. AZZLE ERCASE ONIOUS _____
26. GIO HETE SMA _____
27. DETTA MANE RAB _____
28. AMEL APIA NDA _____
29. ASANT DGERY NTUM _____
30. ANNY AWL RARCHY _____
31. ECILE NIZE UISH _____
32. BUTE OGEN TEENTH _____
33. GREL IGEE OLEON _____
34. ERGO MAGE TOUR _____
35. ATZ HORA ROID _____
36. NTIE TEE TUROUS _____
37. OES OLAR TILUS _____
38. ELNUT PINESS UOUS _____
39. ABOO NEY RAPIN _____
40. GATE SAVA SAW _____
41. LDLY RCHER ROID _____
42. ENTLY ERAGE QUET _____
43. ANDER ERAS RDIAN _____
44. KAJOU LLEN ORAH _____
45. DOCK MEL SELVES _____
46. EWN SBOK VISM _____
47. ISMA JA MIZER _____
48. EGIOUS STERY UAGE _____
49. ADEL MAND NTH _____
50. ORAE RNUM SIP _____

BLANKING OUT 2

See page 7 for instructions.

1.

```
FOR___TU___
___OL_ST___OL
___BARD___E
_I___CT_LIGH_
___BTE___UGE
_H_TE__HAR_
```

Theme: _____

2.

```
D____N_SE
C____OIS___A_HER
RE_____R_TI_G
M____TIM___AW
_UTTE_N___
    SQ_A_H
TRI____OM_T___CA_
___S_R P_IN___R_
HY___C_I___C_L
_L_S_-CON_C_O___
R___B_R BA____
_O_ND_A_E
BR_____R_Y___VE
A____I_AN
    REVOL____N
_ACTR_____MEL
AS____NOM_CA_
    _NIT_
PR_C_A_T___AT_R
____E Z___E
```

Theme: _____

3.

```
_E___E___KI_G
_R_NU___TED
    SU___R
OP_OM_____T
___INT C____ODY
F___A_I_
ES_I___A_E
_EA_ D_W_
_ES___NER
    _R___S
E_____
    H_L__AY_
B_UT CH_____N_
____OU_ M_P
```

Theme: _____

4.

```
FRE___E F___ME
G_O_P___INK
___P_RT___TIE_
___BR___IA
_ARB_R____L
____IO_R_PH_ES
__K_RS WI_D
__R___NG
    NE_D_E
____ ___KEL
__IN___ND
    ___NA
```

Theme: _____

Answer, page 106

ADDITIONAL TEXT

In each of these addition problems, every digit has been replaced with a letter, with the same letter always representing the same digit, as in a cryptogram. (The code changes from puzzle to puzzle.) See if you can make these words add up.

1.
```
    T  U  T  T  I
+ F  R  U  T  T  I
_____
    S  C  O  O  P  S
```

2.
```
    S  A  N  D  S
+   O  A  S  I  S
_____
    D  E  S  E  R  T
```

3.
```
    K  E  R  M  I  T
+ K  E  R  M  I  T
_____
    M  U  P  P  E  T
```

4.
```
    A  L  B  E  E
+   I  B  S  E  N
_____
    A  C  T  I  N  G
```

5.
```
    B  U  G  S
+   B  U  N  N  Y
_____
    R  A  S  C  A  L
```

WHAT'S OUTSIDE A NAME?

Although it may not look like it at first, each of the following words and phrases contains the name of a famous person, reading from left to right. Of course, the names aren't necessarily spelled with consecutive letters, which does make things more difficult, so we've also provided the person's occupation. The first and last names will each be found separately; some letters will be left over (but at least half will always be used), and no letter will be used more than once. For instance, ANGLO-FRENCH (politican) leads to the answer AL GORE (An**GLO**-f**RE**nch). Names are listed in order of increasing total length, but are otherwise unordered.

1. CHALLENGE (director) _____

2. THING OF BEAUTY (actor/comedian) _____

3. MALAYSIAN (architect) _____

4. TIGER MOTH (actor) _____

5. WEBMASTER (actor) _____

6. PROKARYOTIC (entrepreneur) _____

7. MERRYMAKING (actor) _____

8. DARBY AND JOAN (author) _____

9. ETERNALIZES (golfer) _____

10. HARMONISTS (playwright) _____

11. JUGULAR VEINS (artist) _____

12. PRESERVATION (political leader) _____

13. STOMACH ULCER (actor) _____

14. BLABBERMOUTH (athlete) _____

15. GRANDNIECE (author) _____

16. BLUE RIBBONS (author) _____

17. PERIODIC TABLE (actor/comedian) _____

18. METAMORPHOSIS (singer) _____

19. BALKANIZING (comedian) _____

20. RADIATOR VALVE (poet) _____

21. SLEEP LIKE A LOG (director) _____

22. MENTAL BALANCE (voice actor) _____

23. BERNOULLIAN (musician) _____

24. DISADVANTAGE (columnist) _____

25. LIVE AND LEARN (athlete) _____

26. CRYSTALLOMANCY (author) _____

27. STUBBORN-HEARTED (magnate) _____

28. MILES AND MILES (director) _____

29. DARWININAN THEORY (journalist) _____

30. MELODRAMATIZATION (actor) _____

31. MAID OF ORLEANS (writer) _____

32. CHILE CON CARNE (singer) _____

33. THOUGHT-READERS (poet) _____

34. OBLIGATIONARY (political leader) _____

35. WAGE FUND THEORY (actor) _____

36. SUBCONSTELLATION (athlete) _____

37. TRAVELING SALESMAN (actor) _____

38. JUVENILE HORMONES (author) _____

39. SECRETARIES GENERAL (actor/comedian) _____

40. SELF-MAINTAINING (athlete) _____

41. ADJUSTABLE SPANNER (author) _____

42. PHILANTHROPISING (socialite) _____

43. BEARER OF GLAD TIDINGS (singer) _____

44. TRANSMERIDIONALLY (actor) _____

45. POSTAL DELIVERY ZONE (director) _____

TEAMWORK

Everyone loves to see their favorite sports teams mixing it up. In this puzzle, teams whose names share the same place name have gotten together and mixed it up by rearranging the letters from both their names into two new words. For instance, the New York GIANTS and New York METS might pool their resources to make the words STING and TEAMS. Teams will never repeat in the puzzle, though the same location may appear more than once. Teams may come from any major league sport: baseball, basketball (including WNBA teams), football (including CFL teams), hockey, or soccer (MLS or NASL). Can you see through the disguises these teams are sporting?

1. CLINIC BUSTERS _____

2. DISHPAN HOTEL _____

3. WISER HATBOXES _____

4. REALISTIC THREADS _____

5. PLEDGES RIPCORDS _____

6. IGOR LISTENS _____

7. KENNEDY ASSAILERS _____

8. ALDRIN SARCASM _____

9. NOVEL ROSARIES _____

10. SLAPSTICK SARDINE _____

11. LITERATE PRESSES _____

12. SUES TYCOONS _____

13. STAY CROSSBOW _____

14. GIRLY BANTERERS _____

15. PERIL SELFISHLY _____

16. CASHFLOW SANK _____

17. SKEW SCRUBBER _____

18. FISHY ORACLES _____

19. CLOSEST CARP _____

20. SPRINGTIDE SNOWS _____

21. CURBSTONE GONGS _____

22. LIBELS BRASS _____

23. STORK COASTERS _____

24. KASHMIR AWARENESS _____

25. DRAGS PREACHERS _____

26. ENDLESS BRAG _____

27. SWAZILAND RATIONS _____

28. PERMAFROST PAELLAS _____

29. RILES SCANDINAVIA _____

30. CAREENING NIGHTCLUBS _____

31. BRASH HARVESTERS _____

32. RENTS ASTONISH _____

33. SURREALISTS RSVPS _____

34. CINEMATIC PANDAS _____

35. DEFLATES SPAMMERS _____

36. JEWELER CUTBACKS _____

37. ANALYSE SUBJUGATOR _____

38. SMURFS CONSORTED _____

JIGSAW SQUARES 3

See page 12 for instructions.

NEW WORDS
- Color that shares its name with a French liqueur
- *The Producers* won twelve of them: 2 wds.
- Rifle nicknamed "The Gun That Won the West"
- She was abducted by Hades

SQUARE 1
Across
- Like stuffed toys
- Innocent
- 60 minutes past the witching hour: 2 wds.
- Type of organic compound
- Must: 2 wds.

Down
- Actress Turner and *Smallville* character Lang
- "I've got a gun, and I'm not afraid to ___!": 2 wds.
- Give a ring
- Ned's neighborino
- Prevent, with "off"

SQUARE 2
Across
- Down-filled piece of bedding
- Machine used for hoisting
- Honda division
- Help to loosen up again, as the Tin Man
- Masts

Down
- Need defrosting: 2 wds.
- New, to Dante
- Obeys an order to stop
- Political divisions of a city
- Town ___ (reporter of yore)

SQUARE 3
Across
- "Reduce, ___, recycle" (green motto)
- Heavy cutting tools
- Invite to one's apartment, say: 2 wds.
- Heron or shoebill, for example
- Big name in car cargo carriers

Down
- As it were: 2 wds.
- What people who've forgotten their sunscreen might seek
- ___ Gold (1997 Peter Fonda film)
- Vine that covers huge swaths of the South
- Fighting: 2 wds.

SQUARE 4
Across
- Event featuring team roping and barrel racing
- Like unappetizing apples
- Lion of *The Lion, the Witch, and the Wardrobe*
- Item on a PowerPoint slide, perhaps
- ___ ballerina

Down
- Nancy's skating rival
- Domain
- Insult from Bob and Doug McKenzie
- Dwight defeated him in 1952 and 1956
- Problem for a long-distance runner

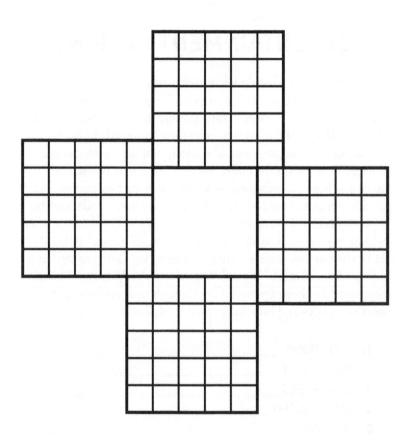

ENTERTAINMENT OPTIONS

Modern culture features a wide variety of entertainment options. Not only can we choose from movies, songs, plays, novels, albums, poems, TV shows, video games, and more, but we also have a wide variety of ways to transform the words in their titles. For instance, we can add a letter, subtract a letter, change a letter, or anagram the entire word. In each title below, each word has been transformed using one of those four methods (a different method for each word), and then those words have been alphabetized. For instance, CARRIER RESIST is *Sister Carrie* after adding a letter to "Carrie" and anagramming "Sister," and GEL MART is *Get Smart* after changing a letter in "Get" and deleting a letter from "Smart." If a title begins with "A," "An," or "The," that word has been ignored. Sort through your options on the next two pages and hopefully you'll be well entertained.

1. ALOE DOME _____
2. ENID HOARDS _____
3. BING PEELS _____
4. MOVE TINTED _____
5. DICE RACY _____
6. NAIVE SONG _____
7. BARD CREAKING _____
8. DANGERS GREW _____
9. LURCH SNAKED _____
10. DROOPERS HARPISTS _____
11. CHICANO HOP _____
12. MERRY MOANS _____
13. LONELY RITZ _____
14. BEADY DEBRIS _____
15. GIANT LOUD _____
16. CINEMA COMET _____
17. BETTER CLARETS_____

18. PROTECT UNWARY _____

19. FIE LEAP _____

20. DYNAMO MAGIC _____

21. BOXES VOLLEY _____

22. REIGNS WELDING _____

23. COMMEND SIMILES _____

24. BODY LONGED _____

25. SWING WET _____

26. CHIEF WRENCH _____

27. CINERAMA PIPE _____

28. ALAN IMPELS _____

29. FOLLOW MEAN _____

30. FAME RESEND _____

31. BENCH CHIN _____

32. BELLY DOMAINS _____

33. STRING TINSEL _____

34. MAIL TESTER _____

35. PAMPER PLANTS _____

36. FINE SPICERS _____

37. FORM MANILA _____

38. BOREDOM IMPERIL _____

39. BLOCKER HUNT _____

40. PAR PORKY _____

41. EVILS INDICATORY _____

42. BIGGER GOD _____

43. EARS PONDER _____

44. POSITRON PROLE _____

45. ACHES HANDOUTS _____

46. MAIN ROYALIST _____

47. LIGHTENERS SOY _____

48. BALD CAMERON _____

49. RIPTIDES SWAY _____

50. ALPHA ONE _____

Answer, page 108

DROPQUOTE/FLOATQUOTE

In a dropquote, columns of letters appear above a blank grid, which will be filled with a quote. Black squares represent spaces between words. (Words wrap around at the end of a line.) Letters drop into the grid within their column, but the order in which they are placed is for you to determine. This puzzle has two quotations, and letters can drop down from above or float up from below. Letters at the top will drop down into the upper grid, and letters at the bottom will float up into the lower grid. Letters in the middle may go up or down; you must figure out which are which. The speaker of each quote is indicated. Enjoy your ups and downs!

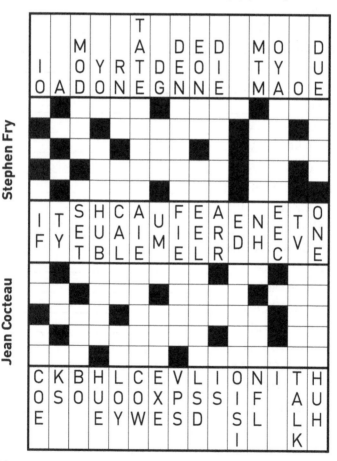

Answer, page 109

BLANKING OUT 3

See page 7 for instructions.

1.
```
B _ _ FR _ _ E
_ R _ _ N _  B _ LL
_ _ S _ IV _ L
EM _ _ O _ D _ R
_ E _ _ Y
   _ _ _ _ LLERY
_ _ _ _ FTNE _ _
S _ H _ O _ _ O _
UNS _ _ _ _ _ _ M _ N _ IKE
   COND _ C _
```

Theme: _____

2.
```
P _ _ _ S _ _ N
_ _ _ _ _ _ SH  OM _ _ _ ET
HO _ _ L
   P _ OP _ _ _ _ TO _
COM _ _ UND
   _ _ _ _ _ _ EST
_ _ DR _ G _ _ _ D
_ _ _ _ _ APS _ BL _
_ R _ N _  CH _ E _
HO _ _ _ _ _ ALI _ E
BRO _ _  FR _ _ _ _
   GR _ U _ _
S _ _ _ L  IN _ _ _ TIN _
_ _ RTS  _ ER
   M _ _ _ _ I _ _
_ EC _ _ _ ARITY
```

Theme: _____

3.
```
A _ C _ N _ _ _ T
DE _ _ _ _ _ AG _
_ E _ T _ _ TIF
B _ _ _ _ _ CA _ _ _ _ _
_ AILK _ _ _ _ ER
_ _ _ _ _ LEX
   FR _ _ _ ION
```

Theme: _____

4.
```
_ _ LE _ D _ _  _ EAR
CHA _ _ _ _ E _ _
   _ _ _ _ CE  _ ANC _
   REVO _ UT _ _ _ _
BURI _ _  _ _ U _ _
_ _ LOW  _ _ _ _ _ AGE
MO _ _ R _  T _ _ ES
_ P _ _ LED  O _ _ _ _
F _ _ _ _ _ N _  NEM _
FAC _ ORY
   W _ _ _ _ _ _ _
_ ID _ FTE _ N _ _ _ _
MU _ IC _ _
   HAR _ _ _ _ Y
_ LODH _ _ _ _ _ _
RI _ _  K _ _ _ _ PI _ S
C _ _ LECT _ _ _ _
   A _ _ _ _ _ ME _ T
_ K _ _ T _ C _ L
```

Theme: _____

CUT IT OUT

Each clue below leads to a two-word phrase in which the two words are nearly identical, except the second one has had a letter cut out. For instance, the clue "Item that won't fit in a fireplace" gives the answer LONG LOG. Clues are presented in ascending order of answer length, but are otherwise unordered. Chop chop!

1. All-encompassing embrace
2. Rock musician's equipment left out in a drizzle
3. Cheer up a young fellow
4. Putt or tap-in, e.g.
5. Groom the hair of Obama's predecessor
6. Well-scrubbed Scottish family
7. Guru did a few laps around the pool
8. Shopping center with only a few stores
9. Undersized adolescent
10. Branch used to see how low some dancers can go
11. Prompt nobleman
12. Extra ship's mast
13. Metal undergarments worn notably by Madonna?
14. Speedy foray
15. Angel's out-of-tune instrument
16. Clothing worn by someone who wants to be alone?
17. Dromedary arrived
18. Cover-up regarding Amelia Earhart
19. Ravi Shankar, for one
20. Shout from underneath
21. Steal the instrument of the guy who plays reveille
22. Bullwinkle in a rather depressed mood
23. One who runs errands for Tiger Woods
24. Well-built reading room
25. Rouge that's more purple than red
26. Stand-up entertainer on the USS *Enterprise*?
27. Visitors play Twenty Questions
28. Animal that can barely wheeze out a whinny

29. Send a grilled cheese sandwich into space
30. Step down from the throne
31. Emotion seen in a famous *Mommie Dearest* scene
32. Masculine, for the most part
33. Figure out that a tennis game is tied
34. Formal insult directed at Scrooge
35. Says, "Those are my bivalves!"
36. Newsletter for the poor
37. The raw power of polka music?
38. Box seen in the funny pages
39. Seeks handbags
40. Most agile man of the cloth
41. Newborns taken care of by Ken's beloved
42. Driver and passengers, all prudently wearing seatbelts
43. List of those that say "cock-a-doodle-doo"
44. Puts some Granny Smiths to use
45. It keeps moviegoers from getting too cold
46. Talk about a decathlon event
47. Intersection where all the officials who examine causes of death are located
48. Two and a half dozen people demanding water
49. Senses the presence of some Eskimos
50. Raising a numbered paddle or nodding, e.g.
51. Amorous gesture that isn't part of a trip to Lovers' Lane?
52. Old agricultural worker who's really quite nice
53. Tapioca that's getting runny and starting to pool
54. Indiana resident who is more particular
55. Series of flashback scenes featuring Romeo and his family
56. Insult that covers a lot of topics
57. More hypodermics than are necessary
58. Atonement made by pirates in an operetta
59. Making a black bird flinch
60. Nicotine, for example
61. Monastery's history and traditions
62. Tool used for piercing someone through the body
63. Slight change in a quarrel

Answer, page 110   41

DOUBLE PLAY

We've taken some two-word phrases whose words begin with the same pair of letters, deleted those letter pairs, and smushed what's left into a single string of letters. For instance, UEOOD started out as the phrase BLUE BLOOD. Can you identify the rest of the original phrases without too much toil and trouble?

1. INLLECTOR _____
2. NETCKSON _____
3. NDIDMERA _____
4. LESITION _____
5. RESTRESS _____
6. JAMARTY _____
7. OGIEARD _____
8. LDENOSE _____
9. IZELENG _____
10. VENTHAL _____
11. UTECENT _____
12. ORTRIFT _____
13. BLLOWAY _____
14. LDSTAGE _____
15. RACLELE _____
16. EENAPES _____
17. DESTUSE _____
18. ANDILL _____
19. UNDBIN _____
20. ASHOOD _____
21. CHAELY _____
22. SSRKET _____
23. ARPENT _____
24. BSONRL _____
25. ELLOCK _____
26. IDRIAN _____
27. TTLELL _____
28. CHMOND _____

42

29.	ITEALE	_____
30.	TCHPE	_____
31.	MMYCK	_____
32.	LLXBY	_____
33.	STUGH	_____
34.	URALT	_____
35.	MANAD	_____
36.	XASCH	_____
37.	DGEDY	_____
38.	ERLLY	_____
39.	ICETE	_____
40.	CECTS	_____
41.	LICOT	_____
42.	ENCHY	_____
43.	SPIST	_____
44.	DIAK	_____
45.	SUGE	_____
46.	LLLE	_____
47.	LONY	_____
48.	VAMP	_____
49.	ANDA	_____
50.	STVE	_____
51.	CHON	_____
52.	BLER	_____
53.	TEVE	_____
54.	NSEY	_____
55.	FEST	_____
56.	BERW	_____
57.	SBOS	_____
58.	GRD	_____
59.	RDT	_____
60.	XED	_____
61.	GER	_____
62.	TCE	_____
63.	DX	_____
64.	BY	_____

INTERNAL AFFAIRS 2

See page 13 for instructions.

1. SICK TETRA _____ ____
   COMB TONE _____ ____
   OATH STEEP _____ ____
   EACH SELL _____ ____
   CEDE PATTER _____ ____
   BURST RATE _____ ____
   PEAL RIPPER _____ ____
   ITEM LEGACY _____ ____
   MAVEN PERT _____ ____
   PINED RUDEST _____ ____
   Bonus: _____

2. OLIVER PRATE _____ ____
   JEEP SWEAR _____ ____
   COME PROMOS _____ ____
   CUPID PORE _____ ____
   ADMIT STALE _____ ____
   ACTION CLAMP _____ ____
   PITY ROMPER _____ ____
   HEED SITAR _____ ____
   COMMENT MINCE _____ ____
   FATS HEMLINES _____ ____
   Bonus: _____

Answer, page 111

CAMOUFLAGE

Each pair of words conceals a phrase or hyphenated word. The first half is hidden in the first word, and the second half in the second word, always in consecutive letters. For instance, OVERAMBITIOUS SPARTACUS contains BIT PART. Can you find all the hidden bits and parts below?

1.	IMPINGE	SPONGEBOB	_____
2.	BRUNETTE	BEWILDER	_____
3.	JUXTAPOSE	ABUNDANCE	_____
4.	AUTOPILOT	SHOGUN	_____
5.	SENTIMENTAL	ARCHIPELAGO	_____
6.	TRUMPETER	COMPANY	_____
7.	AYATOLLAH	SCALLION	_____
8.	HAWKEYE	MILLIMETER	_____
9.	SWINDLE	ARCHIMEDES	_____
10.	ANTIFREEZE	MAGENTA	_____
11.	CHANGELING	CHAIRMAN	_____
12.	KHRUSHCHEV	CAMCORDER	_____
13.	COMPLEXITY	IMPROVISATION	_____
14.	LANDOWNER	LAUNDERETTE	_____
15.	CONCEITED	SOVEREIGN	_____
16.	PSYCHOPATH	GRASSHOPPER	_____
17.	TAUTOLOGY	DURACELL	_____
18.	HEREDITARY	EXPANDABLE	_____
19.	VAUDEVILLE	BATWING	_____
20.	TSUNAMI	EMPHATIC	_____
21.	FLAMENCO	CASSOWARY	_____
22.	STRUMPET	ZOROASTRIANISM	_____
23.	CHOPPINESS	STREETCAR	_____
24.	MICROBIOLOGY	VICEROY	_____
25.	HALLOWEEN	CATECHISM	_____
26.	RIBBONED	MACHINATIONS	_____
27.	MANTICORE	IGNORAMUSES	_____
28.	UNEARTHED	DECONGESTANT	_____
29.	KILOCALORIE	SPHEROID	_____
30.	STUNTWOMAN	ADOLESCENTS	_____

Answer, page 111

STATE DEPARTMENT

You say you're looking for states? Well, you've come to the right department. Let me take a look at the list of words and phrases you've brought. Oh, how convenient, they have enumerations indicating the answer lengths. Yes, we can absolutely add state abbreviations to all of these to make new words and phrases, no problem. For instance, given the word REAP, we could add DC to it to make REDCAP (if only the District of Columbia were a state). A list of clues to all the new words, with a list of states and abbreviations for reference, appears on pages 48 and 49. There aren't any enumerations on that list, but I'm sure you'll have no trouble matching its answers to the ones on the original list (on these two pages). Each state abbreviation is used exactly once.

1. Animal seen with a whale in a famous diorama in New York City's American Museum of Natural History (5)
2. Arrive via transporter, Star Trek–style (6; 2 wds.)
3. Boneless cut of tenderloin (5)
4. "Boola boola," e.g. (5)
5. Bucking mount at a rodeo (5)
6. Car model whose safety in rear-end collisions was criticized by Ralph Nader in the '70s (5)
7. Come together, in a way (8)
8. Commit to the earth (5)
9. Cosecant's reciprocal (4)
10. Dash lengths (3)
11. Either creator of "The Dude" (4)
12. Fabric also known as khaki (5)
13. Final resolution of a plot (10)
14. Foodstuff of mysterious origin (5)
15. Gen Xer's parent, to a Canadian (6)
16. Get ready for bed, perhaps (7)
17. *Hungarian Dances* composer (6)
18. Ingredient in a Gibson or Manhattan (8)

19. Insubtantial (6)
20. It can make captures en passant (4)
21. It might indicate where one lives (6)
22. Kind of beer (6; 2 wds.)
23. Less disorganized (6)
24. Like Randy Savage (5)
25. Middle Earth's Fangorn, e.g. (6)
26. Not likely to rebel (6)
27. Official language of Iran (5)
28. One and only (4)
29. One rolling around in the mud (8)
30. Opposite of supine (5)
31. Owing money (8; 3 wds.)
32. President whose middle name was Gamaliel (7)
33. Printer brand (5)
34. Quatrain in a sonnet, e.g. (6)
35. Roman goddess of agriculture (5)
36. Scrumptious (6)
37. Sing like Al Bowlly (5)
38. Steed or Peel, e.g. (7)
39. Stroll (5)
40. Sunni's counterpart (6)
41. *The Cotton Club* star Gregory (5)
42. Three-pointed sword wielded by the superheroine Elektra (3)
43. Treats poorly (6)
44. Two-dimensional surface (5)
45. Type of animal that Wossamotta U's most famous alumnus is (5)
46. U.S. Army Corps of Engineers worksite of 1904–14 (6)
47. What causes the world to shine like you've had too much wine, in song (5)
48. Where Oedipus ruled as king (6)
49. Word repeated three times in the title of Jules Feiffer's first book (4)
50. Word said when giving up (5)

Alabama (AL)	Louisiana (LA)	North Dakota (ND)
Alaska (AK)	Maine (ME)	Ohio (OH)
Arizona (AZ)	Maryland (MD)	Oklahoma (OK)
Arkansas (AR)	Massachusetts (MA)	Oregon (OR)
California (CA)	Michigan (MI)	Pennsylvania (PA)
Colorado (CO)	Minnesota (MN)	Rhode Island (RI)
Connecticut (CT)	Mississippi (MS)	South Carolina (SC)
Delaware (DE)	Missouri (MO)	South Dakota (SD)
Florida (FL)	Montana (MT)	Tennessee (TN)
Georgia (GA)	Nebraska (NE)	Texas (TX)
Hawaii (HI)	Nevada (NV)	Utah (UT)
Idaho (ID)	New Hampshire (NH)	Vermont (VT)
Illinois (IL)		Virginia (VA)
Indiana (IN)	New Jersey (NJ)	Washington (WA)
Iowa (IA)	New Mexico (NM)	West Virginia (WV)
Kansas (KS)	New York (NY)	Wisconsin (WI)
Kentucky (KY)	North Carolina (NC)	Wyoming (WY)

NEW WORDS

a. Act of public condemnation
b. Alternate name for a cherry pepper
c. Automobile mishap
d. Band with the #1 hit "Set Adrift on Memory Bliss": 2 wds.
e. Bottom-feeder
f. Brought together to a central location
g. Cheerful, good-natured quality
h. Chuck Berry was arrested for violating it in 1959: 2 wds.
i. Crunchy cube in a salad
j. Decompression sickness, familiarly: 2 wds.
k. Delta follower
l. Delta site: 2 wds.
m. Female surfers
n. Friendly
o. Fuel sold by Hank Hill on King of the Hill
p. Gary Larson's strip, with "The": 2 wds.

q.   George who pretended to be named Art Vandelay
r.   Gravely dignified
s.   Hall & Oates hit with the lyric "Watch out, boy, she'll chew you up"
t.   He succeeded Shimon and was succeeded by Ehud
u.   Horror franchise installment of 2009: 2 wds.
v.   *House of Games* characters: 2 wds.
w.   It's about 340 meters per second at sea level: 2 wds.
x.   Large airways in the lungs
y.   LPGA Tour star Juli
z.   Meteorologist's prediction
aa.   More like taffy
bb.   Muscular
cc.   Mushroom featured in Asian cuisines
dd.   Name of Clement Clarke Moore's "jolly old elf," briefly: 2 wds.
ee.   New York subways' aboveground counterparts: 2 wds.
ff.   Pacific Northwest tribe
gg.   Pitcher Don who played his entire career with the Dodgers
hh.   Raze to the ground
ii.   Really run-down
jj.   Reluctant-to-socialize party attendee
kk.   Residence
ll.   Rest up in bed after an illness
mm.   Skedaddle
nn.   Some Formula One engines: Hyph.
oo.   Sticks together
pp.   Subtitle of Frankie Valli's "The Sun Ain't Gonna Shine"
qq.   Sweeping view
rr.   Theoretical trans-Neptunian world sought by Percival Lowell: 2 wds.
ss.   Vague
tt.   Venturing, as a guess
uu.   Well-to-do, well-connected New England residents
vv.   Window that lets the sun in from above
ww.   Woman working on stain removal, perhaps
xx.   Worksite for key grips and best boys: 2 wds.

Answer, page 111   49

TOO MANY QUOTES

This puzzle combines movie trivia and wordplay. Each quote below is really two movie quotes smushed together: the start of one and the end of another. For each, determine the actor who spoke one, and the movie in which the other appeared (these may be in either order). Then combine the beginning of the first source with the end of the second source (the number of letters used from each portion is indicated) to get the final answer. Take "We're gonna need a bigger boat, my dear Watson." The first quote is from *Jaws* (spoken by Roy Scheider), and Basil Rathbone says the second quote (in *The Adventures of Sherlock Holmes*) and JAWs + Basil RathBONE = JAWBONE. Now ... action!

1. That'll do, my dear, I don't give a damn.
    _____ (3) + _____ (3) = _____

2. You had me at a nice chianti.
    _____ (3) + _____ (4) = _____

3. Cinderella story. Outta nowhere. A former groundskeeper, now the last survivor of the Nostromo, signing off.
    _____ (3) + _____ (4) = _____

4. You do not talk about dead people.
    _____ (3) + _____ (4) = _____

5. All right, Mr. DeMille, I'm a golden god!
    _____ (5) + _____ (3) = _____

6. Kiss me. Kiss me as if you're trying to seduce me. Aren't you?
    _____ (4) + _____ (3) = _____

7. Open the pod in the vessel with the pestle.
    _____ (3) + _____ (4) = _____

8. I'm Spartacus! I'll have what she's having.
    _____ (3) + _____ (4) = _____

9. Kneel before kings of New England.
    _____ (3) + _____ (3) = _____

10. Once the bus goes 50 miles an hour, the bomb is armed, but what am I?
    _____ (3) + _____ (4) = _____

11. Soylent green is French fried potaters.

_____ (4) + _____ (3) = _____

12. Stella! Hey, they're here already! You're next! You're next!

_____ (3) + _____ (5) = _____

13. He's not the messiah, he's my little friend!

_____ (4) + _____ (3) = _____

14. You betcha she's my sister! She's my daughter!

_____ (3) + _____ (4) = _____

15. They may take away our lives, but I'm not going to take this anymore!

_____ (3) + _____ (3) = _____

16. Why are frogs falling from the sky? I feel like I'm taking crazy pills.

_____ (4) + _____ (5) = _____

17. Fasten your seatbelts. It's going to stick needles in my eyes.

_____ (5) + _____ (5) = _____

18. You aren't too bright. I like that in a man. Prepare to die.

_____ (3) + _____ (3) = _____

19. There ain't no sanity clause! Be very afraid.

_____ (3) + _____ (4) = _____

20. This is crazy. I finally meet my childhood hero and he's trying to kill us, and most poor suckers are starving to death!

_____ (3) + _____ (4) = _____

21. Nah, I mean, I'm already pregnant, and I'm all out of bubble gum.

_____ (3) + _____ (4) = _____

22. Let me see if I've got this straight: in order to be grounded, I've got to love the smell of napalm in the morning.

_____ (4) + _____ (3) = _____

23. I think people should mate for life, like pigeons or Hitler with a song in his heart.

_____ (3) + _____ (3) = _____

24. In this grave hour, perhaps the most fateful in history, come out, come out, wherever you are!

_____ (5) + _____ (3) = _____

Answer, page 112   51

HALF AND HALF

The words in the left-hand column can each be paired with a word in the right-hand column such that, if you cut each word in half and swap the second halves of the words, you'll get two new words. For instance, given the words TRENCH and BRANDY, you could swap their second halves to make TRENDY and BRANCH. What do you say, are you ready to test your 50/50 vision?

1.	BANDIT	_____	a.	BARLEY
2.	BISHOP	_____	b.	BARQUE
3.	BOTANY	_____	c.	CANDLE
4.	BURGLE	_____	d.	CANINE
5.	CONFER	_____	e.	COMPEL
6.	CRAYON	_____	f.	CORDED
7.	DOCTOR	_____	g.	ENAMOR
8.	EFFECT	_____	h.	ENDURE
9.	FELONS	_____	i.	EXPORT
10.	FLOCKS	_____	j.	GARDEN
11.	FOULER	_____	k.	GAUGES
12.	GRINCH	_____	l.	HEARTH
13.	GUINEA	_____	m.	LITTLE
14.	HUMMUS	_____	n.	MALIGN
15.	MISERY	_____	o.	MARVEL
16.	NATIVE	_____	p.	PALTRY
17.	ORIENT	_____	q.	PAROLE
18.	PARISH	_____	r.	POLKAS
19.	PROFIT	_____	s.	PREFAB
20.	RANCHO	_____	t.	PUNISH
21.	RESTED	_____	u.	RECENT
22.	SENATE	_____	v.	SHAMED
23.	SQUINT	_____	w.	SHOWER
24.	TRASHY	_____	x.	SPLASH
25.	TREBLE	_____	y.	STEPPE
26.	VALIUM	_____	z.	WINTER

Answer, page 114

BLANKING OUT 4

See page 7 for instructions.

1.
```
_ O _ N T   _ E   _ _
_ I _ D   _ I _ _ _ _
_ C H M _ _ _ _ Z
S L A N _   R _ _ _ _ _
D I _ _ _ R _ E
_ _ _ _ _ _ I S K
N _ _ W _ _ I _ _
    W O _ D
_ _ _ R I E D   _ _ _ _ _
_ _ M _ Y   _ I T
V I _ T _ _ _ A   _ _ _
    A L B _ _ T
G R _ _ D _ O _ _ _
_ E L F -
    _ _ _ _ I _ M A T I _ _
_ A L L _ _   A _ G _ _ _
P _ E _ S _ _ _ _ F U _
_ _ D P O I _ _
_ O L D F _ _ _ _ _ _
_ A U L I N _
    _ O _ _ Z _ O V _
_ _ _ _ T E P _ P E R   _ _ N
_ _ _ _ A B R _
R I T _ _ _ _ E   _ A L _ N _
_ E R M _ N
    _ E P U B _ _ _
_ _ L _ A T I _ N   A _ M _
_ _ _ _ K I S H -
    A _ _ _ _ _ _ A N
```
Theme: _____

2.
```
_ _ _ L Y _ _ N
S U _ _ R _ _ N _ A _ E _
_ _ R _ O G R A P _ _
L O _ A L L Y
    E _ C _ I _ _ A N
    _ P _ _ _ E
_ E _ _ G E I _ T
_ I T H _ _ _ _ I A _
E _ T R _ _ _ _ E W A _
_ _ L _ I _ A _ K
S E _ _ _ _ I _ Y   R _ _ K
_ C _ M O _ Z _
_ I A M _ _ _ _   L _ L
S _ _ _ _ L L   L O _ _
_ _ H A _ _ _ E D _ N
C _ _ N _ E R -
    B A _ _ _ _ C E _
_ I R _   S O _ _ _ _ _ O
```
Theme: _____

3.
```
_ _ _ _ _ _ L A U _ E _ _ E
_ _ A B _ _ _ P L E _
F A C T O _ Y   _ _ T _ _ _
    S _ O R _
_ _ _ W   B U _
    _ U R E
_ L _ Y _ N _   D _ _ N
    _ _ _ _ A S Y L _ _ D
```
Theme: _____

CRYPTO-MINIS

Normally, cryptograms are at least a sentence or two long, because without enough text to work with, you don't get enough information about letter patterns to solve the darn things. But sometimes you just don't have time for a full cryptogram, and, well, I figured that's where I could help. I selected some words and short phrases that use exactly 6 or 8 different letters of the alphabet, but they're already half-solved for you! How so? I only enciphered half of the set of letters! (That is, 3 out of 6, or 4 out of 8; the actual number of enciphered letters will vary depending on how many times each of those letters is repeated.) For instance, the phrase CHAIN GANG—which uses the letters A, C, G, H, I, and N—might be encoded as UHXIN WXNW, with the H, I, and N untouched. The letters used as replacements will never be letters that appear in the original word or phrase. The first 20 phrases contain 6 letters; the rest have 8. Now get cracking!

1. K H N   K N S S - K A S N   H N A R K

2. U O U J - U O L J   U L J N N I U

3. R H B B I B O   O A O

4. W R O W H - R S - W R O W H - W R N

5. Q H R N I H   Q R Q I H S

6. F R E N S E S   W N F E R

7. A L U E - A L T T S E S

8. P T O S P T   O S W T L L

9. J O Y Y M J T   J A Y Y

10. FLSTS AFT FTD

11. WYC WYC WVRDVC

12. BLDDLSSLL BIBADS

13. DINDOK BOOK

14. ROME EVMEVNVE

15. LZLLZFRZL TPZ

16. WSOPGSW WSROPGS

17. FGGF KFQEGIGF

18. PNPAMN PYRNNY

19. HRILP CPLRCCIP

20. JDIVD CDJTDI

21. VEEMETVXT LMBRVRMVX

22. HO MGH WE GH WELGHD

23. FRMMPRMFF IB FMATTRM

24. TAYER A CWNRE WNNY

25. IO OCIRCK IO HKN'O PKKPH

26. BONTADETBONA BONTTNES

27. VBSVRYSIY OYEVB

28. CUIF COO FUAGG PAFF

29. SRBUDS BR BRRPURIOU

30. GOL SULLG OLRLAFGLR

31. BRIFBREFFIAZZY

32. MTBLR TMMROO MHTNNRL

33. JEDLIPPLDCE MLD

34. PISHUAN PNAFNSH

35. TYENITPY TOYYPNS

36. DSSDIR OS LWE WEDRL

37. MIHTNATNHESSNT

38. WRTTP WODDTLL DRTLLIPW

39. MYRGS YBTOGBSTTS

40. CRHACHY CO YIVVHR

41. HILLNERAGIE NAGH

42. GTAT MOSSTABTMMY

43. PLATIOR APPIROMLOT

44. LSMP PLNS PVPOSGP

45. TKRTKRRZBPLZTKOR

Answer, page 115

MIXED MESSAGES 3

See page 15 for instructions.

1. AARP FORT THEM WONK ANN THUNKED WON WEALTHINESS ETHER

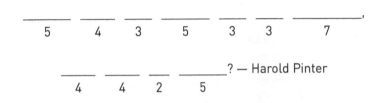

$\underline{\hspace{1cm}}$ $\underline{\hspace{1cm}}$ $\underline{\hspace{1cm}}$ $\underline{\hspace{1cm}}$ $\underline{\hspace{1cm}}$ $\underline{\hspace{1cm}}$ $\underline{\hspace{2cm}}$,
  5   4   3   5   3   3   7

$\underline{\hspace{1cm}}$ $\underline{\hspace{1cm}}$ $\underline{\hspace{0.5cm}}$ $\underline{\hspace{1.5cm}}$? — Harold Pinter
     4   4   2   5

2. WAIL SAY VINES TONIC MAP ANISE DICTION LOUD RUBEN OCEANUS ADE EOWYN LIL

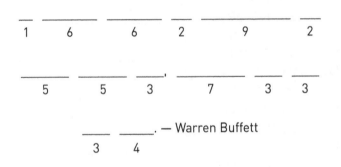

$\underline{\hspace{0.5cm}}$ $\underline{\hspace{1cm}}$ $\underline{\hspace{1cm}}$ $\underline{\hspace{0.5cm}}$ $\underline{\hspace{1.5cm}}$ $\underline{\hspace{0.5cm}}$
  1   6   6   2   9   2

$\underline{\hspace{1cm}}$ $\underline{\hspace{1cm}}$ $\underline{\hspace{0.5cm}}$, $\underline{\hspace{1cm}}$ $\underline{\hspace{0.5cm}}$ $\underline{\hspace{0.5cm}}$
  5   5   3   7   3   3

$\underline{\hspace{1cm}}$ $\underline{\hspace{1cm}}$. — Warren Buffett
  3   4

3. IRON DEBTOR PEARLIER CALEB NO-SEE-UM WALT BAYS FIFED ENTER

$\underline{\hspace{0.5cm}}$ $\underline{\hspace{1cm}}$ $\underline{\hspace{0.5cm}}$ $\underline{\hspace{0.5cm}}$ $\underline{\hspace{2cm}}$ $\underline{\hspace{0.5cm}}$
  2   5   2   2   13   3

$\underline{\hspace{1cm}}$ $\underline{\hspace{1cm}}$ $\underline{\hspace{0.5cm}}$ $\underline{\hspace{1.5cm}}$. — Coco Chanel
  4   6   2   9

Answer, page 116

CHARACTERS WITH CHARACTER

In this list of fictional characters, we've added a little extra character. Specifically, one letter each in their first and last names, anagramming to make new words. For example, Tiny Tim might be represented by the phrase NIFTY MIST. The names have been ordered by total length but are otherwise in no particular order. Can you unscramble them?

1. TEMPER SNAP   _____
2. JENGA LEERY   _____
3. FOILS ANGLE _____
4. MAMET REPEL   _____
5. KABOB THEFT   _____
6. MASK SHAPED   _____
7. MANY CHARMS   _____
8. BORN REPTILE   _____
9. LIBEL KISSER   _____
10. EXALT FELONY   _____
11. FOND PARDNER   _____
12. CAMEO UPWIND   _____
13. FOXIER TRASH   _____
14. MOST PERKILY   _____
15. ALARM FACTOR   _____
16. OBOE ALREADY   _____
17. HERON FLOWER   _____
18. WILDLY AWOKEN   _____
19. PRAYER NOMADS   _____
20. LAXLY CLAMBER   _____
21. POISE ROYALTY _____
22. HATRED ADVERB   _____
23. SVELTE LURKER   _____
24. CHERUB YAWNED   _____
25. ANDROID GRAVY _____
26. URUK-HAI USUAL   _____
27. GOBI THROBBER   _____

28. BOMB CATHARTIC _____
29. DECIDE ONESELF _____
30. HATTER REBUILT _____
31. DASHED ALGEBRA _____
32. HURRAY TREETOP _____
33. LAST APPRAISED _____
34. SMOOCH EARMARK _____
35. LASTLY WEBLOGS _____
36. GARBAGE CAVERN _____
37. BRAYING FEMURS _____
38. FROGGER SAMBAS _____
39. ROMAN CHORALES _____
40. CRIKEY CORRIDAS _____
41. EXERTED ROAMING _____
42. ORIGIN TAXONOMY _____
43. MARYLAND BIKERS _____
44. UPSTART ELLIOTT _____
45. MONOPLANE TOOLS _____
46. RANDOM ODDMENTS _____
47. BROWNIAN TIMBER _____
48. BEANERY BUMBLER _____
49. GERMAN MOPINESS _____
50. COARSE DIAMONDS _____
51. TSUNAMI PROWESS _____
52. OVERUSES PECANS _____
53. AIRFARES FRANCE _____
54. CARNIVORE SWARM _____
55. LENIENT AEROBICS _____
56. SCHNABEL OUTBIDS _____
57. SITUATING LEERILY _____
58. RESONANCE CONCERN _____
59. ERRATIC WASHBOARD _____
60. MOTORHEAD REDBOOK _____
61. TRIATOMIC DADAISM _____
62. WOMANLY MIRTHLESS _____
63. DWARFED THREESCORE _____

Answer, page 116

MISDIRECTION 2

See page 22 for instructions. And even if you don't need to refamiliarize yourself with the rules of the puzzle, don't forget that exactly half the answers will be reversed (in this case, that's 15 out of 30), and that the "opposites" may be reinterpreted misleadingly.

ACROSS

1 Easy-to-carry beer purchase: Hyph.
6 Abyss
9 Tempest creator
10 Red dessert wine
11 Sergeant who wanted "just the facts"
13 Seinfeld's neighbor across the hall
14 Last forever, seemingly: 2 wds.
17 One of a set of eight identical babies
19 More modern version of a record sleeve: 2 wds.
22 Piece heard over the opening montage of Woody Allen's *Manhattan*: 3 wds.
25 Bring to a halt
26 Strong suit
27 Squander
28 Rear ends

DOWN

1 Residue on a candelabra
2 Legendary dancer Duncan
3 Group of lions
4 Kidnap
5 Chanteys, e.g.: 2 wds.
6 Like Desi Arnaz (and many cigars)
7 *La ___ Vita* (Fellini classic)

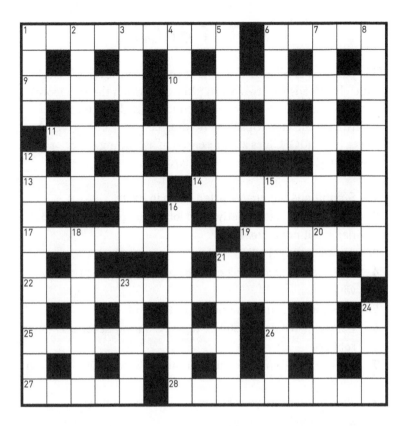

8 Philandering men have them

12 Children's television show that featured Rita Moreno and Morgan Freeman, with *The*: 2 wds.

15 Having lots of bushy hair

16 Watch part that makes 1,440 trips around the dial in a day: 2 wds.

18 Educational level between bachelor and doctor

20 It's swung over a plate

21 Phoenix's role in *Walk the Line*

23 Hypnotizes or bewitches

24 "Damned dirty" creatures in a Charlton Heston film

PUT IT BACK

This puzzle is similar to Cut It Out (p. 40), but reversed. Each of the clues leads to a two-word phrase in which the two words are nearly identical, but the second one has had a letter added. For instance the clue "Spacious holding cell on a ship" gives the answer BIG BRIG. Clues are presented in ascending order of answer length, but are otherwise unordered.

1. Sumptuous banquet scarfed down in haste
2. Mystic who does a pretty good job of sleeping on a bed of nails, but not a *great* job
3. James Dean, in 1955?
4. *America's Funniest Home Videos* host who is surprisingly wise
5. Saucy independent candidate of the '90s
6. Perfect piece de resistance to end a daring *Ocean's 11*–style robbery
7. DNA map for small magical creatures who wear pointy red caps
8. "If you celebrate your birthday, I have to celebrate something too" policy
9. Lifeboat in need of some freshening up
10. Bury legendary playwright Harold
11. Longtime local inhabitant who's easily duped
12. Be green with one's trash
13. Someone who ought to be flying the Angry Roger instead of the Jolly Roger?
14. A sufficient amount for statistical analysis, say
15. Tasty mushroom tidbit
16. Where college kids study *The Stranger* and *The Plague*
17. Horses' stalls that could use some airing out
18. Beat scotch into a froth by hand
19. Listening to oboes and clarinets to soothe one's stomach, e.g.?
20. Spry mountaineer

21. Parsley sprig that tackily sticks out like a sore thumb on the plate
22. Omen that really packs a wallop
23. Breaking someone's habit of overusing profanity
24. Oscar-winning actor Roberto who's completely harmless
25. Serving of magical liquid
26. Firearm anachronistically wielded by a Japanese feudal leader
27. Someone recently baptized in the middle of the night, wearing sunglasses, using a pseudonym
28. College teaching staff that can't do anything right
29. Flip-flop-gate?
30. Windowmaker who's just not as industrious as his coworkers
31. Heron relative with a sour temperament
32. Scoundrels' floating flowers
33. Helps some female relatives get free after a failed escape act?
34. Brings mountain ponies into existence
35. Trash that's sitting in the carport
36. Fury regarding a loss of electrical power
37. Museum displaying images of boats propelled by oarsmen
38. Help out Paul McCartney or Tina Weymouth, say
39. Wear and tear on the Stanley Cup
40. Do something that can't help but be severely criticized
41. What Queen Victoria would wake up with after drinking one too many
42. Talk smack about a New York hockey player
43. Having a squirt gun in one's pocket while approaching airport security?
44. Pink wading bird that is waaaaaay out of the closet
45. Leeward Island dweller who supports disarmament
46. Legendary U.S. general finally giving up the ghost
47. Making fun of one's attempts to prevent heat loss
48. "I've just had a brilliant idea! I should get out of this sudden downpour," e.g.

Answer, page 117

DROPQUOTE/FLOATQUOTE 2

See page 38 for instructions.

Georgia O'Keeffe

Top letter tiles:

I B M	E C O M O	D D	O A P E N	A L A N	P E S T S	E E	M A R T	T O N	H D T V	W H E E	E Y E R	M R R	S E

(solving grid with black squares)

Middle letter tiles:

L Y N	G I F	H I C H	A L E E	O U T	I O S	R A N	I F	L E S	S O T	H A S	F A T E	T H E N	T I E

Will Rogers

(solving grid with black squares)

Bottom letter tiles:

I D J	A U D I	S L I P	T A I R	F I R W	S W A M	A S H	T A R	R N S	G A T E	A S	I R R	T O N S	O R

Answer, page 118

CENTRAL LOCATIONS

The U.S. state capital of Atlanta, Georgia has the word TAG hidden in its middle; similarly, Salem, Oregon conceals MORE. The words below can all be found hidden inside *world* capitals (with the city first and the country second). Can you trace them to their places of origin?

1. LINGER _____
2. RIDS _____
3. MAP _____
4. DAMN _____
5. CRAG _____
6. GRADES _____
7. KARAT _____
8. BLINI _____
9. SARGE _____
10. END _____
11. RULES _____
12. NEST _____
13. OUR _____
14. STROM _____
15. DUNE _____
16. STUN _____
17. ROE _____
18. LAP _____
19. BIKE _____
20. GALA _____
21. CUSS _____
22. REB _____
23. VIAL _____
24. TOE _____
25. ADORE _____
26. ATOM _____
27. GOD _____
28. RESIN _____
29. IF _____

Answer, page 118

JIGSAW SQUARES 4

See page 12 for instructions.

NEW WORDS

- Space cadet
- Roughing it: 2 wds.
- People in confession booths, presumably
- Leopold and Loeb, e.g.
- Deceitful trait
- Laurie of *The Big Bang Theory*

SMALL SQUARE 1

Across
- Any nonzero number raised to the 0th power
- Need for curing olives
- Material for a candy soda bottle

Down
- PC program's file extension
- Animal consulted on the subject of Tootsie Pops
- Word that may prevent passage

SMALL SQUARE 2

Across
- Burrows who cowrote the scripts to *Guys and Dolls* and *How to Succeed in Business Without Really Trying*
- Item holding up a calendar, often
- Monogram associated with New York City's formerly named Triborough Bridge

Down
- Sound surreptitiously made by a medium
- Org. that kept a file on John Lennon
- *Jeopardy!* legend Jennings

SMALL SQUARE 3

Across
- Feeding trough site, perhaps
- Dark and Stormy ingredient
- Org. concerned with greenhouse gases

Down
- "How can I ___ this?"
- Syllables of hesitation
- Rory's love, on *Doctor Who*

SMALL SQUARE 4

Across
- Name of the Baltimore Ravens' mascot
- Key near the space bar
- Ending for web or mini

Down
- Was introduced to
- Tech company once led by Steve Case
- Professional number-cruncher, for short

LARGE SQUARE 1

Across
- The Bard of ___ (Shakespeare sobriquet)
- Picnic problem
- Picnic problem
- Actress Ryan of *Star Trek: Voyager*

Down
- *Star Trek: The Next Generation* empath Deanna
- ___ Fein
- River through Saint Petersburg
- Not completely closed

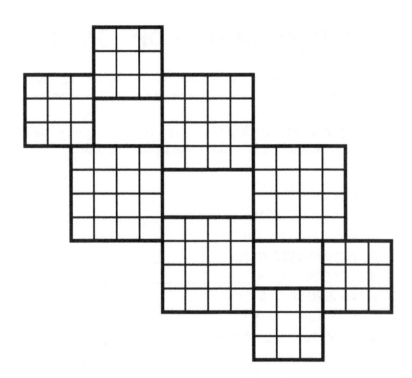

LARGE SQUARE 2

Across
- Exert pressure (on)
- Stare at wolfishly
- German microcar designer Fritz
- Joint ailment once called "rich man's disease"

Down
- Doubly curved archway
- Take care of, as a garden
- Sport with fairways and greens
- ___ Bator

LARGE SQUARE 3

Across
- Amazing accomplishment
- *Six Feet Under* actress Taylor
- Summit
- Do programming work

Down
- Bossy-to-be
- Lit-up sign in a movie theater
- Designer Oscar ___ Renta: 2 wds.
- Sitcom youngster played by the director of *Frost/Nixon*

LARGE SQUARE 4

Across
- Plant used for seasoning
- The Bosporus forms part of its border
- Satellite signal receiver
- Completely caught up

Down
- Morales seen on *Caprica* and *NYPD Blue*
- Converts to MP3, as a CD
- Alternative to a shower
- Tricky to solve

Answer, page 118

ENTERTAINMENT OPTIONS 2

The rules for this puzzle are the same as they were on page 36, but the titles are longer: now they contain three or four words (after discarding leading articles). As before, of the four kinds of wordplay used (adding a letter, deleting a letter, changing a letter, and anagramming), none is used twice in the same title.

1. BIND MINCE THREW _____
2. HOLE LOSE TOTAL _____
3. GOD HAUNTING WILD _____
4. HOSE RUBLES WIDER _____
5. COY DOES HEWN _____
6. ASCEND SOLVES WITCH _____
7. DAIS HOARD THING _____
8. PRIMATE RAN SHAVING _____
9. BLUR SON STUNG _____
10. HAMLET LOUSE SAND _____
11. CLANG DUAL SANE _____
12. SLIDE STONY WET _____
13. NOTE ROD TOKEN _____
14. AREN'T ERECTS MOAN _____
15. GOODS THICKEN WIDE _____
16. ASLEEP LEASE MEN _____
17. BET FEATHER SNOWS _____
18. GONG ONE THAWS _____
19. FEE NUDER SIN _____
20. CLUES SETTER SHILL _____
21. BING FELLOW TAX _____
22. NET RAVE WORD _____
23. FLOOD LOGGING SAG _____
24. EVEN OFF TEAS _____
25. FORM SHIFT THEM _____

26. HAD LOCO LURE _____

27. BOOS MAORI SUPPER _____

28. BAND FAKERS WEEKS _____

29. ON PHONY TRACK _____

30. LAOS RIDES SHUN _____

31. CROPS HOST SNUB _____

32. LOSE OMEN WIN _____

33. BENCH PSALM TYROS _____

34. DRY STAINED WILL _____

35. SHOUT WINE YES _____

36. AMY RATION STEVEN _____

37. DROWN HACK LACK _____

38. COLA LAUGHTER MINDERS _____

39. JILL MOBY VREELAND _____

40. EGRETS MISTS OBIS _____

41. DRYEST GAIN TIDES _____

42. DANTE HALL OWE _____

43. FIENDS LAND NEARBY _____

44. COO ONE VAT _____

45. BEAR IDOLS MEAL _____

46. GIN MANGO PARS SALT _____

47. ABORT CHUM FADO NOTING _____

48. ALLY HEWN HURRY MELT _____

49. ION LOO RANGE SACK _____

50. ADMIRER GO LEGGY SURE _____

51. BET FINDERS GILL MAY _____

52. FOILED GAIN GENT TOWN _____

53. BEG BROOD ETHER ILL _____

54. FIT HOW LIE MOE'S _____

55. FOLD LIE SMITE STEMS _____

56. ELATING FILBERT HATS PAGER _____

57. BYE DEPTH PROD TON _____

58. ENTIRETY FROG HER TOY _____

MIX-INS

In each of these puzzles, the first two clues provide a set of letters that produce the rest of the answers. The letters of the first clue's answer are the "ingredients"; the letters of the second clue's answer are the "mix-ins." The rest of the answers are words derived by adding the mix-ins one at a time to the ingredients and anagramming. For instance, if the first answer were ART and the second answer were PEN, the letters P, E, and N could each be added to ART and anagrammed to make the words TARP, TEAR, and RANT (which would appear in the puzzle in that order, matching the spelling of the mix-in word).

1. Dreck _____
   Like activities shown in beer commercials _____
      Don't attempt to stop _____
      Illicit downloader _____
      The Birthday Party playwright _____
      It gets you most of the way home _____
      Fool's gold _____

2. Coruscant or Hoth, e.g. _____
   "Spare me the ___ details!" _____
      Fabric around a calf: 2 wds. _____
      Cornmeal dish _____
      Box outside a window, perhaps _____
      Possible cause of yard repossession? _____

3. Leave an aftertaste _____
   They're affected by accelerandos _____
      Part of a moppet's hairdo _____
      In a daze _____
      Creature who messes with machinery _____
      Singular potato chip? _____
      Lear's eldest daughter _____
      Night Gallery host _____

4. Get down pat _____

Word before "peas" on bumper stickers _____

    Most welcoming _____

    Bolt's Rhino, for one _____

    Diana's counterpart _____

    Seat divider at a cinema _____

    Fred Flintstone's boss: 2 wds. _____

    Word before clam or trunk _____

    Stung _____

5. Heavy _____

Formal order _____

    Depression treatment?: 2 wds. _____

    Hero's love _____

    Subject of a barbershop standard _____

    How one might prefer one's elbows: 2 wds. _____

6. Totally confident _____

Slaves away _____

    Have a conversation, say _____

    Six-day event of the Bible _____

    Lickety-split: 3 wds. _____

    Klezmer instrument _____

    Less demure _____

7. Intensifier before "cold" or "deaf" _____

1991 John Goodman comedy: 2 wds. _____

    Souvenirs _____

    Like some tech support: Hyph. _____

    Petrarch work _____

    Pool worker, for short _____

    Flexor's counterpart _____

    Makes amends _____

    Hot _____

    Restriction for some apartments: 2 wds. _____

    Square _____

8. Like roles in Broadway revivals _____

"Kiss my ___!" (*M*A*S*H* line): 2 wds. _____

    "My Best Friend's Girl" band: 2 wds. _____

    It's used to prevent rings _____

    Disperse _____

    Word before fever or letter _____

    As blue as can be _____

    Optical ranges _____

    Fat ___ (Kirstie Alley series) _____

9. Like some tofu _____

Room that holds the cassocks, albs, etc. _____

    Absolute temperature scale units _____

    Leather material, possibly _____

    Like a digitally published book _____

    Knackwurst feature?: 2 wds. _____

    Fixes, as a broken URL pointer _____

    View often seen in souvenir snow globes _____

10. Place info may be stored on a card _____

Tool used by Rodin _____

    Bench presses work them _____

    One wearing an ironic T-shirt, probably _____

    Having had a few more cocktails _____

    Keep at it _____

    Break _____

    Doesn't hold back: 2 wds. _____

11. Aldebaran, for one: 2 wds. _____

Chide publicly, say _____

    Specialty involving graphics layout: 2 wds. _____

    Eyebrow grooming option _____

    Specialist in Shakesperean drama _____

    One of a set that might think alike: 2 wds. _____

    Put down _____

Answer, page 119

INTERNAL AFFAIRS 3

See page 13 for instructions.

1. BRAT NAIVE _____ ___
   RAM SQUISH _____ ___
   REMARK TEETER _____ ___
   OLD PESTER _____ ___
   MANY TRIMS _____ ___
   MAR NERVE _____ ___
   FORE OOPS _____ ___
   ARMY SPENT _____ ___
   DIED SHOVEL _____ ___
   Bonus: _____

2. INERT TROY _____ ___
   MINUTE NOD _____ ___
   GRANT WAY _____ ___
   DEIFY MOST _____ ___
   METAL TILE _____ ___
   ERA HAMMOCK _____ ___
   IMPLY RODENT _____ ___
   DID VIDEO _____ ___
   SHED UNBAR _____ ___
   Bonus: _____

Answer, page 120

STRIKE THREE

Each of these words and phrases has had three identical letters struck out. (Spacing and punctuation has also been removed.) For instance, SAEAX is STATE TAX with the three T's removed. Can you get the wayward characters back in the game?

1. BEARELAY _____
2. FROENPIA _____
3. EADONCO _____
4. SUERTIE _____
5. INALOER _____
6. HOREENE _____
7. INEORIA _____
8. IANPALO _____
9. STURNLI _____
10. ISTICUS _____
11. IDOSALK _____
12. SOYBOO _____
13. CIUAUA _____
14. ABITAY _____
15. IGOPES _____
16. COWEED _____
17. ESPILO _____
18. AREATE _____
19. CALIER _____
20. KERULE _____
21. EGAPEA _____
22. SLAHAY _____
23. ITTEAY _____
24. AKETAK _____
25. WISIES _____
26. IRUSAT _____
27. LUTWAE _____
28. ANIRUS _____
29. NANTES _____

30. OLIPIT _____
31. AURAY _____
32. MMBER _____
33. AERCU _____
34. COIDO _____
35. DABDA _____
36. AYOOM _____
37. PTROS _____
38. BIFOD _____
39. ITEDO _____
40. SIHTA _____
41. FULDR _____
42. EDOVE _____
43. DOMIS _____
44. FOTIA _____
45. ALBKE _____
46. SUINT _____
47. IVIEN _____
48. ERAWA _____
49. CIAMO _____
50. DOYBA _____
51. IYPHU _____
52. HABAU _____
53. BEABS _____
54. SIROO _____
55. SNONM _____
56. ATUIL _____
57. SLEMI _____
58. OOSEE _____
59. SILEO _____
60. IUISO _____
61. CHAER _____
62. SRIOS _____
63. ATAK _____
64. UABY _____
65. DAMN _____

Answer, page 120

MIXED MESSAGES 4

See page 15 for instructions.

1. VERSE AXLE SAUCERS WALE SLAY SECS VINO
CHANTING NEON

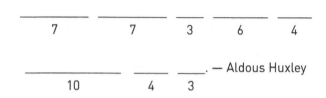

_____ _____ ____ _____ ____
    7   7   3   6   4

_____ ____ ____. — Aldous Huxley
     10   4   3

2. HOMES WOO THOR LIBELER FOAM SUDAN INFO FAT
SUMO BILL TONE RIO SOU

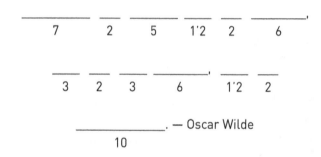

_____ ___ _____ ____ ___ _____,
   7   2   5   1'2 2   6

___ ___ ___ _____, ____ ___
 3   2   3   6   1'2 2

_____. — Oscar Wilde
    10

3. I'D ENSNARER VIG OMENS LINTY METH DID CELL
BASSES YAW FOYER NEGEV

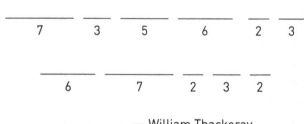

_____ ____ _____ _____ ____ ___
   7   3   5   6   2   3

_____ _____ ___ ___ ___
  6   7   2   3 2

_____. — William Thackeray
   7

Answer, page 121

BAD PAIR DAY

Every word and phrase in this puzzle contains two adjacent identical pairs of letters, like LU in LITTLE LULU or SO in SO SORRY—but each entry in the left-hand column has had those adjacent pairs swapped with those of one of the entries in the right-hand column, with any spaces closed up (so the aforementioned phrases might appear as LITTLESOSO and LULURRY). Can you repair the pairs?

1. ABOBOAL		a.	ALOFOFTER
2. ACTIBABARB		b.	ARARON
3. ASLULUE		c.	BIBIYA
4. BECOCOMS		d.	BROUNINI
5. CANCUCU		e.	BUDDRERETEM
6. CONFYSYS		f.	CHBEBEHAN
7. CRATAT		g.	CISISONIC
8. CRUGUGAPER		h.	COLLORORRAD
9. DIASASIC		i.	DEDELE
10. DROPOPINE		j.	ELYEYELY
11. EDEDATE		k.	EURAMAM
12. FRENNENEEF		l.	HETETHOT
13. GOMAMAF		m.	HONOININ
14. IMPAPANG		n.	HORGIGINSE
15. KOAKAKEF		o.	JAGGULULGE
16. LALANTO		p.	LILIBES
17. LAZILIL		q.	MAUSOSOMS
18. LEHAHAST		r.	MEMEKERS
19. LYLYCRY		s.	OCHCHSS
20. MAPOSOSAF		t.	OPTYTYDED
21. MIDADAUP		u.	PLEPEPLY
22. MILJUJUTER		v.	PRIFIFYPE
23. PASICICUX		w.	RETSISICKET
24. PETENENRANT		x.	REWAWAOP
25. PEYOYOON		y.	ROVEVENK
26. SCOTOTAN		z.	SMIMI
27. SEGEGITY		aa.	SUSULINK
28. STOSTSTY		bb.	TATAMBER
29. TASKOKOST		cc.	TETEMO
30. TAVUVUMPT		dd.	TITIMA
31. THIROROT		ee.	VIRTULELE
32. TOPOSESEO		ff.	XEXEZELA

SKELETON THREES

Each mini crisscross grid contains three words that form a set—for instance, TOM, DICK, and HARRY (though they wouldn't fit into a grid very well, since none of them have any letters in common). Each grid has a few letters filled in to start you off; the remaining letters are below.

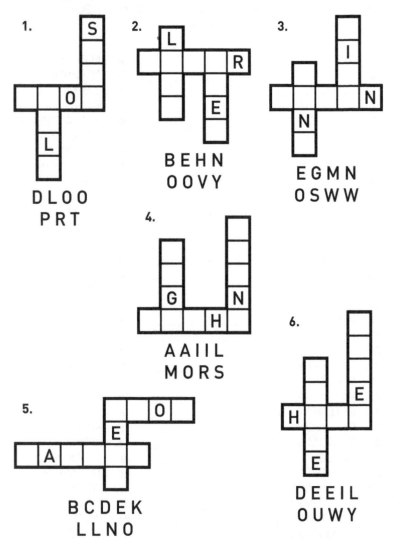

1.

S
O
L

DLOO
PRT

2.

L
R
E

BEHN
OOVY

3.

I
N
N

EGMN
OSWW

4.

G   N
H

AAIIL
MORS

5.

O
E
A

BCDEK
LLNO

6.

E
H
E

DEEIL
OUWY

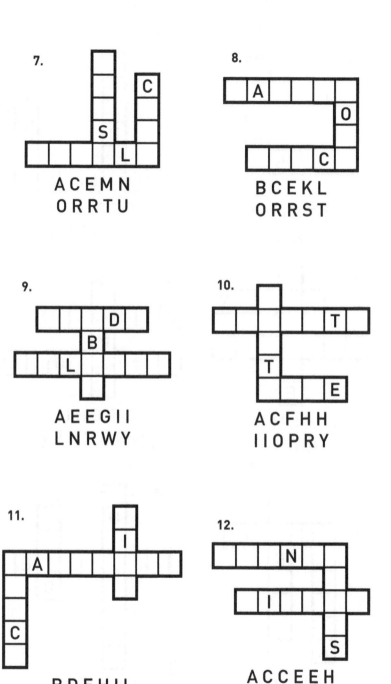

7.

ACEMN
ORRTU

8.

BCEKL
ORRST

9.

AEEGII
LNRWY

10.

ACFHH
IIOPRY

11.

BDEHIL
NORRTW

12.

ACCEEH
KNRRTV

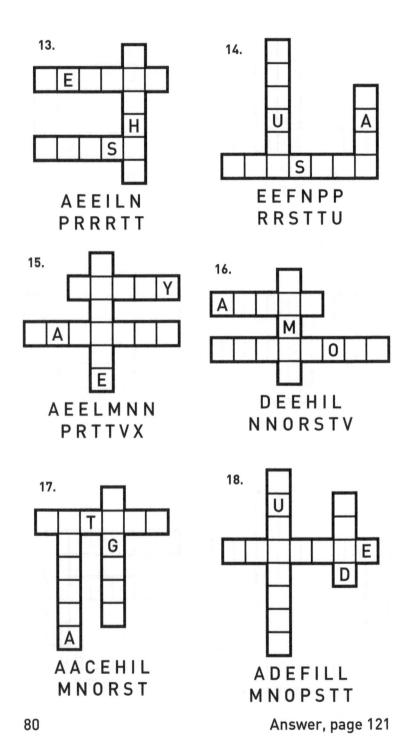

13.

A E E I L N
P R R R T T

14.

E E F N P P
R R S T T U

15.

A E E L M N N
P R T T V X

16.

D E E H I L
N N O R S T V

17.

A A C E H I L
M N O R S T

18.

A D E F I L L
M N O P S T T

Answer, page 121

BLANKING OUT 5

See page 7 for instructions.

1.
```
W _ N D O _ S _ _ _ _
U _ S _   M _ _ _ O R
_ _ _ _ _ S _ _ V _ _ I A
    A V _ N U E
_ _ A _ T H   S _ A
T _ _ _ _   _ A C H _ _ _ _
_ _ B _ A _ T A R
E _ _ _ C _ R O N _ C
    _ U _ _ _
_ _ R _ _ _
    _ V E _ B O A R _
M O _ _ _ C H _ O M _
    D I S _ _ _ A _
K U _ _ _ _ _ I
_ _ G G _ _ N G   _ C T
H _ P _ R _ E N S _ _ _ _ Z E _
_ _ B B _ - _ O X E R
I N _ _ _ _ N _ _ _ Y
_ _ C R O _ U R G _ _ _ _
_ P E L _ _ _ _ _ _ _
_ _ R _ A T _ _ _ E _
```

Theme: _____

2.
```
_ R _ _ _ I D E N _ _ _ A _
    R _ S I D E _ _ _ _
_ I S E _ C _ E
_ _ _ _ _ L Y   _ A M _
_ _ C _ _ _ _ L O N
```

Theme: _____

3.
```
R _ O _ G A _ _ _ Z _
B A _ _   _ U _ H
W O R _   P _ _ _ _ _ _
_ _ _ _ _ E   _ O T T _ _ _ Y
T H _   A _ A _ _ _
_ _ _ _ U N D   C O _ _ _ _
N E _ _ _   _ O _ _ E
_ O I L _ R M _ _ _ _ _
_ _ T _ _ A L _ R I A _
_ _ _ M B I _
U N _ E _ _   _ H _
    W _ A _ _ E R
_ _ _ U _ D _ _ _ _ D
_ _ _ Y   O R _ _ _ S O _
M O _ _ _ _ R
    _ _ _ _ _ _ R Y
_ E R _   M _ S _ E L
N _ N _ E _ U L _ _ _
G O R _ _ _ _ _ _ L A
```

Theme: _____

4.
```
A U _ _ _ C _ O U _ L _
_ M P _ _ _ _ O N
G _ _ _ O M _ M _ N
P _ _ _ S   _ H _   B A _
P _ S T E _   _ _ _ _ L _
_ _ _ _ S S _ _ _ T   _ A W
E _ _ _   W A _ L _ _ _ H
```

Theme: _____

WHAT'S THE CONNECTION?

For each of the phrases below, find a phrase or compound word that can be inserted between the words to complete two more phrases or compound words that begin and end with the given words. For instance, with the starting phrase MICROSOFT STATION, you would insert WORDPLAY to make MICROSOFT WORD and PLAYSTATION. Now start thinking about linking!

1. SWIZZLE SKATING _____
2. CONSTRUCTION WOODS _____
3. CHOCK PYTHON _____
4. SLOPPY SPANIEL _____
5. HOLLAND QUEST _____
6. CREAM LONGLEGS _____
7. MANHOLE JACKET _____
8. PARKING SESSION _____
9. GLOBAL SAVANT _____
10. CLARIFIED FISHING _____
11. SPEAKER OFFICE _____
12. OSCAR CORNERS _____
13. IRON WAITING _____
14. SCOTCH CHAIR _____
15. FACTORY SANITIZER _____
16. QUALITY AGENCY _____
17. SHOUTING SCARED _____
18. ORANGE SALAD _____
19. GREASY CRUMBS _____
20. HIDING SUN _____
21. ACORN DISASTER _____

22. FIRING KEEPERS _____

23. FORTUNE MASH _____

24. PAJAMA SCOOPER _____

25. BUMPER JOCK _____

26. EVASIVE SANDWICH _____

27. SHELTERING FIDELITY _____

28. FATTY SLICKER _____

29. BAKING PEN _____

30. PLEA LADEN _____

31. SLOT SHY _____

32. VENETIAN PALM _____

33. SERGEANT CRUST _____

34. CARGO BAGEL _____

35. POWDER CORRECTED _____

36. SUDDEN CHAMBER _____

37. DISCO WITNESS _____

38. CHEAP JAW _____

39. EAR GENERATION _____

40. WHISTLE CAKE _____

41. BEEFSTEAK NINE _____

42. CREATURE DEFENSE _____

43. PENNY ANT _____

44. ADVERTISING CURVE _____

45. PROVING ROBIN _____

46. CORNER LAUNDERING _____

47. CALVIN NECK _____

48. SINCERELY JAR _____

49. TACKLE WAX _____

50. BODY SURFING _____

MISDIRECTION 3

See page 22 for instructions. Once again, remember that exactly half the answers will be reversed (in this case, that's 15 out of 30), and that what constitutes an "opposite" is often interpreted rather loosely.

ACROSS

1   Competitor of Skippy and Jif: 2 wds.
9   Kuwait or Qatar, governmentally speaking
10   Pending: 2 wds.
11   Piglet's house in the Hundred Acre Wood, e.g.
12   Summer camp overseer
14   Smoothing out
15   Ewer
16   The P of A&P
18   Flying object in an old screen saver
21   Prague or Phnom Penh
23   Sound from Fido
25   Golfer Ernie
26   Indiana Jones is afraid of them
27   What the Tesla Roadster runs on

DOWN

1   Game akin to billiards and snooker
2   Game akin to reversi
3   German art song
4   It may be bid in Bordeaux
5   Takes the lead: 2 wds.
6   The Kennedy administration, figuratively
7   Ella Fitzgerald, famously, e.g.
8   Adhere

13 Like the lesser of two evils

15 Ticket puncher on a train

16 "If you'd be so kind"

17 1963 Cary Grant/Audrey Hepburn film, or item acted out in a party game

19 How one might make coffee first thing in the morning

20 One observing Lent or Ramadan

22 "That ___ part of the deal!"

24 One cooking food with an Indian spice that contains turmeric

Answer, page 123

SMALL CHANGE

Similarly to Cut It Out (p. 40) and Put It Back (p. 62), the clues in this puzzle lead to two-word phrases with a wordplay-style relationship. This time, the only difference between the words is that a single letter has been changed. For instance, the clue "Pooch that doesn't bark" leads to the answer MUTE MUTT. Clues are once again presented in increasing order of answer length (a system endorsed by the Clue Club).

1. Oversized Olympic sled
2. Change that isn't really happening?
3. Home on a mountaintop, perhaps
4. Take a stand against things gradually getting worse
5. Women's magazine that doesn't want to take a firm stance on anything
6. Simply love the building material often used in Santa Fe
7. Craze for shows like *The Sopranos* and movies like *GoodFellas*
8. Extremely concise poem
9. Point of concern that isn't concise at all
10. Bedsheets with stripes
11. Gungans' home planet, which it's simply forbidden to even mention
12. *Ghostbusters* or *Beetlejuice* or the like
13. Brings someone born on April 1 before a judge
14. Not that playful water mammal, the one next to it
15. "A Study of Venom's Effects at Different Altitudes" or "Identifying Poisons by Scent," e.g.
16. Opt to leave North Dakota's largest city out of one's itinerary
17. Is selected above all other suitors?
18. Short puff piece in the newspaper about giant cephalopods
19. Walk-on role for Joe, the cigarette spokesanimal
20. Climb up the Statue of Liberty's hair, say?
21. Prepared microwave meals while in the altogether

22. What the rhythm guitarist plays between the verses
23. Museum worker that's pretty good, I guess
24. What "male" is, goose-wise
25. Item used to play the xylophone in *Swan Lake*
26. Steers clear of anything egg-shaped
27. Noise made by NASA launches
28. A really dull prizefight
29. Officers who say, "Please, sir, would you be so good as to allow me to read your rights to you"?
30. Place that's covered with grapevines and snowbanks?
31. Basic, plain item of headgear for a nun
32. South American cowboy who's always making breaches of etiquette
33. Less severe water damage
34. Relax somewhere that you can't smell the stench
35. Lectern that will explode if it gets wet
36. "Gross, this tastes like Clorox!"
37. That amazing thing over thataway
38. Trading some home-grown produce for a haircut, e.g.
39. Observant Jew dancing at a punk rock concert
40. Friendly disagreement
41. What might result in a perfect score for Greg Louganis
42. License that allows you to live in a cave by yourself
43. The only clergyman that didn't fall in the lake
44. "There's no grits like mom's," e.g.
45. Came out of a store empty-handed
46. Peanut farmer, or president, or diplomat and humanitarian, depending on the era
47. One who can't show his face around the church district
48. How some wire service reporters' computers connect to the Web
49. Cattle thief who's more out of practice
50. Villains' lair that's decorated just horribly
51. Amount in a *City Slicker* star's bank account
52. Particular window treatment
53. Finds flaws

54. What's used to mail a ransom note?
55. Soaps up some people in the tub
56. Proves the nonexistence of safe havens
57. Buddhist artwork used to meditate upon a former South African president
58. Section of a romance novel with fewer sex scenes?
59. Awe a female ruler
60. Letter that's, like, 500 pages long
61. Rioters after a Manchester United victory, for example
62. Abstaining from bagels, matzo balls, kugel, lox, rugelach ... all of it
63. Thunderous applause in response to a speech
64. Follow every answer on the witness stand with "if you must know" or "you stupid lawyer," say
65. Claim to be skilled
66. Cardigan knit out of licorice, vis-à-vis one made of yarn
67. Has security keep an eye on the customers
68. A safe direction to walk if you don't want anyone to pick a fight with you?
69. 15%-off deal for certain noblemen
70. Giving up granny squares for good
71. Checkpoint with less friendly border guards
72. One giving cyanide to a cellmate
73. Seemed to be mollified
74. Ring that Gollum used to be obsessed with before this one?
75. Making off with the silver
76. Toni Morrison, V.S. Naipaul, Gabriel García Márquez, or Ernest Hemingway, e.g.
77. Fine distinctions, such as whether a band was grunge or nu metal
78. Downward trend in the number of con games
79. Give a pep talk to a celeb's hangers-on
80. Serving as a means of communication for a child left in place of another by fairies, at a seance
81. Paper that's under a paperweight, hopefully

Answer, page 123

DROPQUOTE/FLOATQUOTE 3

See page 38 for instructions.

Somerset Maugham

Letter bank (top):

W		F	I	F		H		O	T	I		H	
E	O	A	O	O	O	I	P	W	H	N	T	E	U
A	O	N	H	X	U	N	H	L	E	T	M	E	K
R	S	S	I	Y	E	T	S	S	E	O	C	E	
Y				V					O				

Jerome K. Jerome

Letter bank (middle):

M	C	O	B	C	T	M	C	E	A	L	S	A	T
A	U	U	Y	C	E	O	O	E	O	I	E	A	R
S	T	T	E	R	A	N	N	P	L	L	E	A	E
H	I					T				Y	K	H	N
	E										S		T

Letter bank (bottom):

I	L	A	U	S	G	E	L	D	S	T	I	C	F
R	E	L	N	E	U	X	L	E	T	H	I	O	R
E	T	T	H	T	E	A	L	W	O	U	I	O	Y
		O	I		S	L		Y	P	S			
					S	T							

Answer, page 124

89

SOUND OFF!

You'll need to think ear-rationally to solve this puzzle. Each of the words on this page can be paired with one of the words on the opposite page to make a new word by combining them *phonetically*. (The words are presented in order; that is, the words on this page will always come before the words on the opposite page.) However, one word in each pair has one extra phoneme, which must be deleted; that phoneme will always be the first or last sound in its word. For instance, the words ARK and CHAIN can be combined to make the word ARCANE after deleting the initial "ch" sound in CHAIN. The blanks on the next page indicate the enumerations of the new words formed (listed in alphabetical order), followed by the number of syllables in the word. Now hear these!

1.	ANTICS	16.	DISK	31.	PICKER
2.	ASH	17.	EQUAL	32.	PLAGUE
3.	ASK	18.	FAIL	33.	PLAN
4.	BARRACK	19.	GOSSIP	34.	PRUNE
5.	BASH	20.	HEIRESS	35.	PURSE
6.	BEAU	21.	KNOCKED	36.	SASH
7.	BELOW	22.	LAMB	37.	SERB
8.	BISQUE	23.	LIQUOR	38.	SHAM
9.	BITE	24.	MANNA	39.	SHARP
10.	BULL	25.	MARMOT	40.	SPA
11.	CATTLE	26.	MELANIE	41.	TAUPE
12.	COKE	27.	MIFF	42.	TRIPPED
13.	CORE	28.	MUNDANE	43.	TRUE
14.	CYNIC	29.	PARISH	44.	WHARF
15.	DIP	30.	PARODY	45.	WINTER

a.	ACHE	p.	FREED	ee.	PEACOCK
b.	BOLOGNA	q.	FROWNED	ff.	QUARK
c.	BOOT	r.	ICE	gg.	SICKLE
d.	BUDDHA	s.	ITALIAN	hh.	SKIN
e.	CANAL	t.	JET	ii.	SOAP
f.	CHAIR	u.	JOURNAL	jj.	STREET
g.	CHICK	v.	KNOCKS	kk.	TEA
h.	CLUSTER	w.	KNOTTY	ll.	THANKS
i.	COLLIE	x.	LAID	mm.	TRICKED
j.	CORINNE	y.	LEWD	nn.	TRUCE
k.	CRESCENT	z.	MEANDER	oo.	VALENCE
l.	DESK	aa.	MIST	pp.	WALL
m.	EAGER	bb.	MYRRH	qq.	WEIGHTED
n.	EURO	cc.	NICOTINE	rr.	WISH
o.	FAULT	dd.	PAINT	ss.	YAP

_____ (7, 4)	_____ (9, 4)	_____ (9, 3)
_____ (7, 3)	_____ (10, 3)	_____ (8, 3)
_____ (10, 4)	_____ (8, 2)	_____ (11, 4)
_____ (7, 2)	_____ (7, 3)	_____ (7, 2)
_____ (9, 3)	_____ (8, 3)	_____ (10, 3)
_____ (9, 4)	_____ (9, 3)	_____ (10, 2)
_____ (9, 3)	_____ (10, 3)	_____ (9, 3)
_____ (9, 3)	_____ (9, 2)	_____ (9, 2)
_____ (7, 3)	_____ (8, 3)	_____ (10, 3)
_____ (8, 3)	_____ (9, 3)	_____ (8, 3)
_____ (7, 2)	_____ (9, 3)	_____ (12, 3)
_____ (8, 3)	_____ (10, 4)	_____ (8, 2)
_____ (9, 2)	_____ (8, 2)	_____ (9, 2)
_____ (10, 2)	_____ (9, 3)	_____ (8, 3)
_____ (8, 2)	_____ (6, 2)	_____ (7, 2)

JIGSAW SQUARES 5

See page 12 for instructions.

NEW WORDS

- Weapons used for dramatically opening certain bottles: 2 wds.
- How a stereotypical diva behaves

SQUARE 1

Across

- Patrick Ewing, before he became a SuperSonic, e.g.
- What happens there, stays there
- Moorehead who played Endora on *Bewitched*
- Piece of furniture for Delacroix's reclining odalisque
- Striped relative of the giraffe

Down

- "I Don't Want to Be" singer DeGraw
- Fails to float
- Ensign Chekov's preferred drink, on *Star Trek*
- ___ out a living (just getting by)
- At a healthy clip

SQUARE 2

Across

- The ___ Brothers (*Camp Rock* stars)
- Gets better
- She's asked "When will those clouds all disappear?" in a Rolling Stones song
- "There's no basement at the ___!" (*Pee-Wee's Big Adventure* line)
- Udon alternative

Down

- Rani's husband
- Features that Ernie and Grover have, but Cookie Monster and Oscar the Grouch don't
- Japanese comic books
- Messages with a "reply all" feature: Hyph.
- How Burgess Meredith finds himself in a famous *Twilight Zone* episode

SQUARE 3

Across

- Broods angrily
- ___ barrel (in a tough position): 2 wds.
- This clue contains six of them
- Country singer McEntire and others
- Count up, as bananas on a banana boat

Down

- Bygone teen magazine whose first issue featured articles such as "Losing Your Virginity" and "How to Flirt"
- Talk like a cowhand
- ___ Person in the World (former segment of *Countdown With Keith Olbermann*)
- One fighting the Empire, in *Star Wars*
- First secretary of Health, Education, and Welfare ___ Culp Hobby

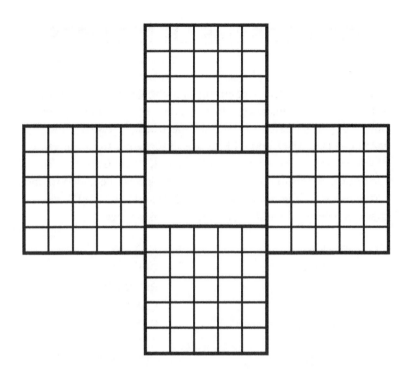

SQUARE 4

Across

- Rusty who racked up 500 hits with each of four different baseball teams
- "It ain't no ___ sit and wonder why, babe" (Bob Dylan lyric): 2 wds.
- Winner of the final heat
- One deciding between PG and R
- Site of Arizona State University's largest campus

Down

- Official investigation
- Had a rendezvous: 2 wds.
- It's between the earth's troposphere and its upper mantle
- '80s action show with the catchphrase "I love it when a plan comes together," with *The*: Hyph.
- Careless swiftness

Answer, page 125

I'VE GOT SOME LITTLE LISTS

Each set of words and phrases on these two pages has something in common. What that something is, though, may not be apparent at first glance. For instance, GROOVY, BIG, and YOGI are spelled only using initial letters of the color spectrum (ROYGBIV), and MASTERED, PLUSH, and GLEAN are all surnames from the game of Clue with one sound changed (Mustard, Plum, Green). Also, each of the words in the box on the next page can be added to one of the lists—so if you saw the words BRIO and NIGHT (White) in that box, you would add them to the two lists above.

1. THREE
   FOREIGN
   TENOR
   STRAY
   STRICTER

2. ESCORT
   LOGS
   LEAGUE
   VACUUM
   ARROW

3. CHILD
   GOOSE
   ADDENDUM
   TOOTH
   CRISIS

4. AMPERSAND
   MILLINER
   GALLOPING
   PINAFORE
   YARBOROUGH

5. AMTRAK
   DELILAH
   REVISION
   LLAMAS
   ROMAINE
   RESEAL
   STRAPPED
   GENIUS

6. STEALING
   BOREDOM
   ALIMENT
   SLUMBERED
   BOTANY
   TRUSTEE
   ABASHED

7. COMMENCE
   DEMOTED
   LAWYER
   CENSUS
   TREACLE
   EGOIST

8. BOLLIX
ELIMINATE
ADVIL
MIDDAY
SERVICING

9. GHOSTLY
AILMENT
BEEFIEST
CLUMSY
ACCIDENT
TAILORS
DEFIANT
BELLHOPS

10. ICE PICK
TORI AMOS
PEPSI-COLA
ENPLANE
EMBERS
TOPIC
GUILT
FELON
CHIRRUP

11. CHERRY
REBEL
SAY
YUMMY
PERHAPS
SUGAR
MONDAY

12. CORNMEAL
FUGUE
DRAGGED
BEAUTIFY
MOUSE
GLACIER
RATION
FINANCE
GREENGAGE

13. DATEBOOK
MIKE RATLEDGE
STAGE MOTHER
WHISPER
SQUAT
NIELS BOHR

EXTRA WORDS

a. ACHILLES **e.** EMERGED **j.** PROFIT
b. CLAMBERING **f.** HEIGHTS **k.** RUSH
c. CRITERION **g.** MOPPED **l.** SANDFLY
d. DRIBBLE **h.** PATOIS **m.** THEREON
i. PEMMICAN

CELEBRITY DOINGS

Everyone loves knowing what the stars are up to! My crack team of reporters has been keeping a close eye on what various luminaries are doing (or what they did). Given these short news items, your job is to find a word that, if respaced (and possibly pronounced differently) could serve as a short headline for that news item. For instance, "Politician Gore tells a fib" could be more concisely stated as ALLIES (Al lies). Each anwer will start with a name (either first name or last name) and end with a verb. One answer is hyphenated.

1. Actress Arthur runs a little three-card monte scam
2. Lawman Wyatt sharpens his knives
3. Actor Waterston tries to get gold from a river
4. Pianist Emanuel was in charge
5. Singer Irene walks nervously back and forth
6. Comedian Buttons went on a whitewater trip
7. A former Princess of Wales wrote some poetry
8. Actor Gary had some dinner
9. Critic Siskel gave movies thumbs up or thumbs down
10. Cellist Yo-Yo doesn't tip the waiter
11. Singer DiFranco finds a life partner
12. Cartoonist Oliphant violently protests in the street
13. Architect Maya gets a move on
14. Comedian Short exists
15. Sportscaster Gowdy wasn't feeling too well
16. Artist Peter uses a chat program on his computer
17. Actress Thompson removes her hat
18. Producer Prince imitates a cow
19. Playwright Dario storms around in a fury
20. Author Stoker showed evidence of a knife wound
21. Actress Gia shakes her tailbone
22. Soccer player Chastain sloughed off a layer of skin
23. Choreographer Hermes irons his trousers with a sharp fold
24. Statesman Thant provides accolades
25. Tennis player Ivan proceeds in a relaxed way

Answer, page 127

INTERNAL AFFAIRS 4

See page 13 for instructions.

1. LAP MACHO _____ ___
   MINT SCREW _____ ___
   LOBO TOOTH _____ ___
   LARGE MAY _____ ___
   FOOTING REEK _____ ___
   DOLL ORBS _____ ___
   KEG STRAY _____ ___
   PAIN RIFF _____ ___
   Bonus: _____

2. ARDENT CRY _____ ___
   ASTER WAND _____ ___
   COLA ORATOR _____ ___
   DEAL TRIDENT _____ ___
   PALE PITAS _____ ___
   FLING GRETEL _____ ___
   PEON STAG _____ ___
   INFER WELD _____ ___
   ANTIC TARP _____ ___
   Bonus: _____

3. GNU POINT _____ ___
   BALL NERO _____ ___
   PET STOLEN _____ ___
   PLEAT SAX _____ ___
   CLONE INGOT _____ ___
   ROPES PLED _____ ___
   POSTER STERN _____ ___
   PAN THOSE _____ ___
   Bonus: _____

Answer, page 128

THEM'S FIGHTING WORDS

In this puzzle, there are no black squares; words are entered end to end with no space between them. Clues are presented by row and column in order of entry in the grid, but the dividing points between answers are for you to determine. Sometimes you'll find two answers in conflict—their intersecting letters won't match. Help those fighting words resolve their differences by replacing the conflicting letters with a different letter that makes new words in both directions (in one case, a proper name). Circle the new letter, and after the grid is completed, read all the circled letters from left to right to reveal what one might do after solving an entire book of word puzzles; then, read them again from top to bottom to reveal what one who loved word puzzles enough to solve that book would do in that situation.

ACROSS

1 Making a speech
  Illegible handwriting
2 Amorous skunk Pepe: 2 wds.
  Words before a testimony
  Jai ___
3 Spotted wildcats
  ___ d'etre
4 Garments in two baseball
    team names
  Sign up for a class, to a Brit
  Govt. security: Hyph.
5 Painter's cover-up
  Thin cut
  Rolls back, as the tide
6 Major Iberian river
  Online message that
    requests an RSVP
  Word before John or
    departed
7 Per ___ expenses
  Shutterbug's purchase,
    perhaps
  Frequent Bacall costar,
    familiarly

8 Static on the screen
  ___ de France
  Lots of money, slangily
9 Having a frog in one's
    throat
  Recycling containers
  Detail-oriented, but not in a
    good way: Abbr.
10 To whom a muezzin's
    prayers are directed
  Pendulum's path
  It hides a pea in a con
    game
11 Nora Ephron's sister (and
    sometime screenwriting
    collaborator)
  George who played Sulu on
    Star Trek
  "___ Mir Bist Du Schön"
12 Yoko who lives at the
    Dakota
  Easy as pie
  ___ Bator
13 Was uncertain
  Sportscaster Dick

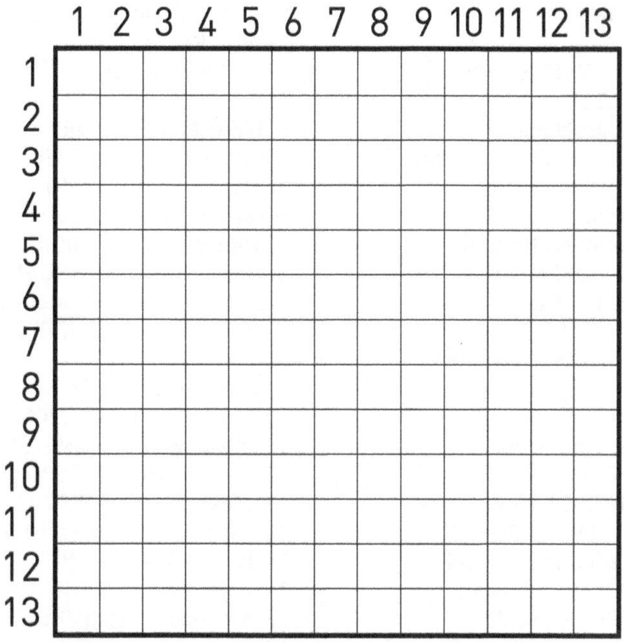

Grid: 13×13 blank crossword grid with columns numbered 1–13 across the top and rows numbered 1–13 down the side.

DOWN

1 Practiced good dental hygiene, in a way
Follow, private eye–style

2 Giving another part, perhaps
Songstress Horne

3 Summit
Cookie that's the subject of "Weird Al" Yankovic's song "The White Stuff"
Give the thumbs-up to

4 Verizon or T-Mobile
Laud

5 Picture on a desktop
"Milkshake" singer
Musical featuring "Good Morning Starshine"

6 "I'm ___ at liberty to say"
Celebrate
Words on a Wonderland cake: 2 wds.

7 Pump purchase
A cattle rustler might try to change its appearance

8 Orch. section with violins
Top-ten tunes
"You talkin' to me?" taxi driver Travis

9 Serf, to a lord
Like soldiers in camouflage, so they hope

10 Ruined, as a parade or a picnic: 2 wds.
Loser

11 Not to mention
"I ___ your pardon!"
Repeated word in the *Macbeth* witches' chant

12 Desire
Combat a leaky boat
Cloudless

13 What actors must memorize
Just-sprouted plant

Answer, page 128

99

7 BLANKING OUT
1. Ivy League schools
BORROWING (Brown)
SYLLABLE (Yale)
PENTAGON (Penn)
PROVINCETOWN (Princeton)

2. Bowling terms
FIRMAMENT (frame)
STRIP POKER (strike)
ALLEGEDLY (alley)
SHOPLIFTER (split)
SOPHIA LOREN (spare)

3. Soda brands
FASHIONISTA (Fanta)
DYSPEPSIA (Pepsi)
SOUTHEAST ASIA (Shasta)
SEMIPRIVATE (Sprite)
FIRE ESCAPE (Fresca)
HAIRDRESSER (Hires)
CINEPHILE (Nehi)
BAROQUENESS (Barq's)

4. *The Brady Bunch* kids
APPETIZER (Peter)
MATRICIDAL (Marcia)
ADJACENT (Jan)
GRUELING (Greg)
ABSORBABILITY (Bobby)
ELECTION DAY (Cindy)

5. Musicals
MACRAME (*Mame*)
GRANDNIECE (*Annie*)
CATALYST (*Cats*)
BINARY NUMBER (*Barnum*)
CARBON DIOXIDE (*Candide*)
CALAMINE LOTION (*Camelot*)
CAREER COUNSELING
    (*Carousel*)
LOCH NESS (*Chess*)
COMPLACENCY (*Company*)
LEVIATHAN (*Evita*)

CIGARETTE CASE (*Grease*)
OLIVE DRAB (*Oliver!*)
PREGNANT (*Rent*)

8 OVERLAP OF LUXURY
1. hypnotic notice (HYPE)
2. marital Ritalin (MAIN)
3. caramel melts (CARATS)
4. printer interior (PRIOR)
5. nuclear clearance (NUANCE)
6. nethermost thermostat (NEAT)
7. remove verse (REMORSE)
8. rusty style (RULE)
9. spell "pellet" (SET)
10. shyster hysterics (SICS)
11. meadow downer (MEANER)
12. respect pectin (RESIN)
13. reckless lesson (RECKON)
14. headwind dwindled (HEALED)
15. flask askew (FLEW)
16. bayou youth (BATH)
17. messiest siesta (MESA)
18. Dublin bling (DUG)
19. dashiki king (DASHING)
20. paired Airedales (PALES)
21. Bacardi cardinal (BANAL)
22. stable blend (STAND)
23. lethal halter (LETTER)
24. single inglenook (SNOOK)
25. tantric trick (TANK)
26. armor morgue (ARGUE)
27. curate atelier (CURLIER)

10 UNDERGROUND FILM
   ## FESTIVAL
1. *Psycho*, (Vera) Miles; tiPSY
   CHOrus, sMILE Seductively
2. *Giant*, (James) Dean; junGIAN
   Therapist, maDE A New
3. *Marty*, (Ernest) Borgnine;
   sMART You, BORG NINE
4. *Casino*, (Sharon) Stone;
   maraCAS IN Order, hiS TONE-
   deafness

5. *Ishtar*, (Warren) Beatty; drumBEAT TYpically, wISH TARzan

6. *Amadeus*, (Tom) Hulce; witH ULCErs, nauseA MADE USe

7. *Zelig*, (Woody) Allen; haZEL IGnored, smALL ENglishman

8. *Chicago*, (Richard) Gere; psyCHIC A GOlfer, roGER Ebert

9. *The Sting*, (Robert) Redford; cloTHES TINGed, geaRED FOR Dancers

10. *Avatar*, (Zoe) Saldana; rehearSAL DAN Always, crAVAT ARound

11. *Crash*, (Don) Cheadle; paniC RASHly, frantiC HEADLEss

12. *Fargo*, (William H.) Macy; oF ARGOnauts, froM A CYclops

13. *Patton*, (George C.) Scott; shoP AT TONy's, men'S COTTon

14. *Traffic*, (Benicio) del Toro; concerT RAFFI Can, yoDEL TO ROomfuls

15. *Gigi*, (Leslie) Caron; nasCAR ONly, drinkinG I GIggle

16. *Vertigo*, (Kim) Novak; extroVERT I GO, casaNOVA Knows

17. *Superman*, (Christopher) Reeve; shiatSU PERMANent, moRE EVEntually

18. *MASH*, (Sally) Kellerman; i'M ASHamed, rathsKELLER MANagement

19. *Aladdin*, (Robin) Williams; sALAD DINner, WILL I AM Sorry

20. *Ghost*, (Patrick) Swayze; thiS WAY ZElda, charminG HOSTess

21. *Salt*, (Angelina) Jolie; banJO LIEs, thiS ALT-rock

22. *I Robot*, (Will) Smith; caIRO BOTh, ostraciSM I THink

23. *Shane*, (Alan) Ladd; balLAD Doesn't, puniSH AN Eardrum

24. *Titanic*, (Leonardo) DiCaprio; wasn'T IT A NICe, comeDIC A PRIOrity

25. *Star Trek*, (Zachary) Quinto; START REKnitting, manneQUIN TOday

26. *Cabaret*, (Michael) York; picniC A BARE Torso, unseemlY OR Kinky

27. *Top Hat*, (Ginger) Rogers; sTOP HATing, pRO-GERShwin

28. *El Cid*, (Charlton) Heston; muscatEL CIDer, smootHEST ONe

29. *Alien*, (Sigourney) Weaver; deniAL I ENter, oWE A VERy

30. *Ransom*, (Rene) Russo; lutheRANS OMit, choRUS SOmetimes

31. *Red River*, (John) Wayne; moRE DRIVERs, highWAY NEed

32. *Twister*, (Helen) Hunt; witH UNTrained, requesT WISTERia

33. *Get Smart*, (Steve) Carell; toxiC ARE LLama, nugGETS MARTha

34. *Home Alone*, (Daniel) Stern; gazpacHO MEAL ON Easter, eaSTER Night

35. *Dangerous*, (Bette) Davis; frenzieD ANGER OUSted, ousteD A VISigoth

36. *Tortilla Flat*, (Spencer) Tracy; acTOR TILL A FLATtering, exTRA-CYnical

37. *Charade*, (Cary) Grant; kellogG RAN The, suCH A RAD Entrepreneur

38. *Sayonara*, (Marlon) Brando; esSAY ON ARAchnophobia, weB RANDOmly

39. *Gaslight*, (Ingrid) Bergman; iceBERG MANgled, makinG A SLIGHT

40. *Shutter Island*, (Mark) Ruffalo; grasS HUT TERI'S LANDlord, gRUFF ALOof

12 JIGSAW SQUARES

```
        S H A W
        E A C H
        M A N E
P H A R I S E E
L U B E     Z A P S
U G L I     I S A Y
S E E N     N E R F
        V I N E G A R Y
        E V I L
        N O N S
        T R E E
```

13 INTERNAL AFFAIRS

1.
O(BLITE)RATE = E
NONE(XISTEN)T = X
T(URPENT)INE = P
DI(SCERN)ED = E
SP(LURG)ED = R
PLAN(CHETT)E = T
DO(GHOUS)E = S
FOR(MULA)TE = A
DE(MOLISH)ED = M
DI(SPENS)ARY = E
PAR(AMOUN)T = N
Bonus: EXPERTS AMEN =
EXPER(IMEN)TS

2.
CH(OPST)ICK = P
SE(PULCH)ER = L
V(OLUNT)ARY = O
STE(PLADD)ER = D
CON(TRATE)NORS = T
H(OMEW)ARD = W
UNC(OUP)LE = O
Bonus: PLOD TWO PL(YWO)OD

14 PRODUCT REPLACEMENT

1. FOREORDAIN; Oreo, Lorna Doone
2. DISSERTATION; Serta, Tempurpedic
3. ULTIMATUMS; Tums, Rolaids
4. INDOLENT; Dole, Chiquita
5. AUDIENCE; Audi, Ford
6. ASPARAGUS; Ragú, Prego
7. SUBPAR; BP, Chevron
8. DEVIANCE; Evian, Aquafina
9. HIERARCHY; Era, Tide
10. EXORBITANT; Orbit, Stride
11. CLOTHBOUND; HBO, Starz
12. APERTURE; Pert, Suave
13. MEMENTOS; Mentos, Certs
14. SPINACH; Spin, Vibe
15. METAZOIC; Tazo, Lipton
16. DIALECT; Dial, Level
17. BORDELLO; Dell, IBM
18. ATAVISM; Avis, Alamo
19. DEFENDING; Fendi, Prada
20. OCCASION; Casio, Omega
21. HARBINGER; Bing, Ask
22. GOALPOSTS; Alpo, Cesar
23. BARCAROLE; RCA, GE
24. MATRIXES; Trix, Life
25. PICOMETER; Comet, Ajax
26. TELEVISE; Levi's, Diesel
27. MONIKER; Nike, Puma
28. TRUFFLES; Ruffles, Wise
39. OCELOT; O-Cel-O, S.O.S
40. HARPOON; Harp, Bass

15 MIXED MESSAGES

1. Never interrupt someone doing what you said couldn't be done.
2. A celebrity is one who is known to many persons he is glad he doesn't know.
3. The first requirement of a statesman is that he be dull.

16 RHYME TIME

1. Talk is cheap.
2. Time marches on.
3. Haste makes waste.
4. Love conquers all.
5. Knowledge is power.
6. Form follows function.
7. Loose lips sink ships.
8. Monkey see, monkey do.
9. Been there, done that.
10. Once bitten, twice shy.
11. Practice what you preach.
12. Lightning never strikes twice.
13. Let them eat cake.
14. Go west, young man.
15. Let sleeping dogs lie.
16. Easy come, easy go.
17. Troubles come in threes.
18. Beggars can't be choosers
19. Still waters run deep.
20. Cold hands, warm heart.
21. There's no place like home.
22. Time waits for no man.
23. Beauty is only skin deep.
24. Many hands make light work.
25. Dead men tell no tales.
26. Where there's smoke, there's fire.
27. Water seeks its own level.
28. Parting is such sweet sorrow.
29. You can't fight City Hall.
30. Look out for number one.
31. Good fences make good neighbors.
32. Actions speak louder than words.
33. Time flies when you're having fun.
34. All that glitters is not gold.
35. Faint heart never won fair maiden.
36. Rules were made to be broken.
37. What goes up must come down.
38. Good things come to those who wait.
39. Many are called but few are chosen.
40. You scratch my back, I'll scratch yours.

18 FLIPPERS

1-x. SEPARATE
2-aa. CRASHED
3-ee. ERASURE
4-hh. AERATOR
5-s. ASHRAM
6-j. BANDAGE
7-dd. BARONETS
8-a. GARBAGE
9-i. SUBDUE
10-ff. RETRACTABLE
11-o. TRUCKING
12-p. DUODENAL
13-bb. FLESHY
14-jj. MALFUNCTION
15-d. WELFARE
16-r. FOLDEROL
17-z. GAMETES
18-b. GANGLIA
19-u. HEARTEN
20-e. KINETIC
21-ii. PALTRY
22-h. LEOTARD
23-gg. SEMANTICS
24-t. NORSEMAN
25-y. RAPSCALLION
26-m. SERAPHIM
27-v. RAMEKIN
28-g. SKILLED
29-n. POTSHOT
30-l. NUTSHELL
31-f. MUSCLING
32-w. SEMITONE
33-c. SPARTAN
34-k. TWINKLE
35-q. DRAWLED
36-cc. WHITECAPS

19 JIGSAW SQUARES 2

F	R	E	T				
L	A	V	A				
A	M	E	N				
	G	A	N	G	L	I	O	N

T	B	A	R			I	P	S	O
A	L	G	A			M	O	H	R
F	A	U	N			E	D	A	M
T	H	A	T	C	H	E	R
			R	U	D	I
			A	L	E	C
			B	U	N	K

20 TOO MANY NOTES

1-w. "Black Dog," Led Zeppelin
2-hh, "La Bamba," Ritchie Valens
3-l. "Great Balls of Fire," Jerry Lee Lewis
4-o. "Believe," Cher
5-d. "Creep," Radiohead
6-x. "Beast of Burden," The Rolling Stones
7-m. "Eleanor Rigby," The Beatles
8-f. "Karma Chameleon," Culture Club
9-cc. "Bye Bye Love," The Everly Brothers
10-p. "Stand by Me," Ben E. King
11-e. "Basket Case," Green Day
12-aa. "Raspberry Beret," Prince
13-ff. "Chain of Fools," Aretha Franklin
14-a. "Maybellene," Chuck Berry
15-j. "Dreams," Fleetwood Mac
16-h. "Good Vibrations," The Beach Boys
17-b. "Hotel California," The Eagles
18-k. "Faith," George Michael
19-c. "Changes," David Bowie
20-t. "Genie in a Bottle," Christina Aguilera
21-ee. "Wannabe," Spice Girls

22-g. "Tears in Heaven," Eric Clapton
23-i. "Call Me," Blondie
24-v. "Sabotage," Beastie Boys
25-r. "Vogue," Madonna
26-n. "Subterranean Homesick Blues," Bob Dylan
27-z. "Comfortably Numb," Pink Floyd
28-s. "Enter Sandman," Metallica
29-q. "Heartbreaker," Pat Benatar
30-gg. "Lady Marmalade," Labelle
31-u. "Once in a Lifetime," Talking Heads
32-y. "Bohemian Rhapsody," Queen
33-bb. "Panama," Van Halen
34-dd. "Waterfalls," TLC

22 MISDIRECTION

G	A	T	S		C	O	R	S	A	G	E	S
E		R			N		E		R		T	P
R	A	E	B		E	R	U	S	A	E	L	P
M		S		C		A		S		B		A
A	B	S	A	L	O	M		A	G	E	N	T
N			A		P		L		C			
Y	D	D	E	R	F		S	G	N	I	L	S
		E		K		S		E				A
S	T	I	N	G		R	O	Y	B	E	A	N
S		R		A		O		E		S		T
E	E	R	T	B	A	R	C		Y	O	G	A
H		A		L		R				O		F
C	O	M	P	E	T	E	S		S	G	G	E

1-Across: STAG (Doe)
8-Across: BEAR (bull)
9-Across: PLEASURE (*pain*)
13-Across: FREDDY (Jason)
15-Across: SLINGS (arrows)
21-Across: CRABTREE (Evelyn)
24-Across: EGGS (Bacon)
5-Down: EYEGLASSES (contacts)
6-Down: ICEBERG (titanic)
14-Down: MARRIED (single)
17-Down: ERRORS (*Corrections*)
18-Down: CHESS (checkers)
20-Down: GOOSE (duck)

24 ODD AND EVEN

1-o. AARDVARK
2-z. TAILSPIN
3-q. MATERIAL
4-v. DIVORCES
5-r. PRALINES
6-d. FLATTERY
7-e. FOOTHOLD
8-w. SLOBBERS
9-t. ROADSIDE
10-k. CABERNET
11-m. FOREHAND
12-j. CERBERUS
13-b. LEFTMOST
14-g. COLONIST
15-a. AUSPICES
16-y. PONTOONS
17-u. PELICANS
18-p. MUSTANGS
19-aa. ROADWORK
20-x. TEN-SPEED
21-n. SEAPLANE
22-i. SOBRIETY
23-f. TOREADOR
24-h. CHLORINE
25-c. TERRACES
26-s. TELEPLAY
27-l. DOMINEER

25 MIXED MESSAGES 2

1. Whenever a fellow tells me he's bipartisan, I know he's going to vote against me.
2. International sport is war without shooting.
3. One must have a heart of stone to read the death of Little Nell by Dickens without laughing.

26 ON WITH THEIR HEADS

1. COMMITTEE (combust, mitzvah, teenage)
2. PERFORMER (perhaps, foreign, meringue)
3. ASPARTAME (asphalt, artisan, amethyst)
4. PARABOLAS (parfait, abolish, lasso)
5. HORSEPLAY (horizon, separate, layette)
6. CABLEGRAM (caboose, legume, rampage)
7. ALABASTER (alacrity, bassinet, terminus)
8. FLAKINESS (flagrant, kindred, essayist)
9. PROPELLOR (proxy, pelican, lorgnette)
10. SPACESHIP (spatula, cesspool, hippo)
11. VENERABLE (venomous, erasure, bleakly)
12. ZINFANDEL (zinnia, fantasy, deluxe)
13. BURLESQUE (burrito, lessened, question)
14. PLAINTEXT (plasma, integral, extremist)
15. WARMONGER (warmth, moniker, gerbil)
16. SPEARMINT (spelunk, armada, intuition)
17. GREENROOM (gremlin, enrollee, oompah)
18. DESPERADO (destiny, period, adornment)
19. BUMBLEBEE (bumpkin, blemish, beefeater)
20. SNAKESKIN (snazzy, kestrel, kingdom)
21. WASTELAND (wasabi, tellurium, androgyny)
22. MAHARISHI (mahogany, aridity, shiatsu)
23. COMPENDIA (comatose, penguin, diadem)
24. MULTIPLEX (mulligan, tipsily, lexicon)
25. BEDFELLOW (bedazzle, felonious, lowercase)
26. MACADAMIA (machete, adagio, miasma)

27. SCAVENGER (scarab, vendetta, germane)
28. CARTILAGE (caramel, tilapia, agenda)
29. QUADRUPLE (quantum, drudgery, pleasant)
30. SCRUNCHIE (scrawl, uncanny, hierarchy)
31. IMBROGLIO (imbecile, roguish, lionize)
32. TRIUMPHAL (tribute, umpteenth, halogen)
33. PERSIMMON (perigee, simoleon, mongrel)
34. CONUNDRUM (contour, undergo, rummage)
35. AMPERSAND (amphora, ersatz, android)
36. MOUSETRAP (mountie, settee, rapturous)
37. SCHNAUZER (scholar, nautilus, zeroes)
38. HAPHAZARD (hazelnut, happiness, arduous)
39. JITTERBUG (jitney, terrapin, bugaboo)
40. FRICASSEE (frigate, cassava, seesaw)
41. SEAWORTHY (searcher, worldly, thyroid)
42. BOULEVARD (bouquet, leverage, ardently)
43. GUACAMOLE (guardian, cameras, oleander)
44. KINSWOMEN (kinkajou, swollen, menorah)
45. POMPADOUR (pommel, paddock, ourselves)
46. STRATAGEM (strewn, atavism, gemsbok)
47. MELATONIN (melisma, atomizer, ninja)
48. BLUEGRASS (blustery, assuage, egregious)
49. COMPLICIT (command, plinth, citadel)
50. STEGOSAUR (sternum, gossip, aurorae)

28 BLANKING OUT 2
1. Detergents
FORTITUDE (Tide)
CHOLESTEROL (Cheer)
GABARDINE (Gain)
SUBTERFUGE (Surf)
WHITE SHARK (Wisk)

2. Shakespearean characters
DIAGNOSE (Iago)
CHAMOIS LEATHER (Hamlet)
RECALIBRATING (Caliban)
MARITIME LAW (Ariel)
BUTTERNUT SQUASH (Brutus)
TRIGONOMETRICAL (Goneril)
LASER PRINTERS (Laertes)
HYPOCRITICAL (Portia)
CLASS-CONSCIOUS (Cassius)
ROBBER BARON (Oberon)
POUND CAKE (Puck)
BROTHERLY LOVE (Othello)
AMERICAN REVOLUTION (Mercutio)
BACTRIAN CAMEL (Bianca)
ASTRONOMICAL UNITS (Troilus)
PROCRASTINATOR (Orsino)
TIME ZONE (Timon)

3. Video games
PEACEMAKING (Pac-Man)
GRANULATED SUGAR (Galaga)
OPTOMETRIST (Tetris)
JOINT CUSTODY (Joust)
FM RADIO (Mr. Do!)
ESPIONAGE (Pong)
TEAR DOWN (Tron)
DESIGNER DRUGS (Dig Dug)
EASTER HOLIDAYS (Asteroids)
BRUT CHAMPAGNE (Rampage)
CONTOUR MAP (Contra)

4. Books of the Old Testament
FREEZE FRAME (Ezra)
GROUPTHINK (Ruth)
EXPORT DUTIES (Exodus)
AMBROSIA (Amos)
HARBOR SEAL (Hosea)
HAGIOGRAPHIES (Haggai)
JOKERS WILD (Joel)
DARNING NEEDLE (Daniel)
GENE SISKEL (Genesis)
MAINLAND CHINA (Malachi)

29 ADDITIONAL TEXT
1. 61664 + 791664 = 853328
2. 78617 + 58707 = 137324
3. 382790 + 382790 = 765580
4. 14366 + 93562 = 107928
5. 9362 + 93445 = 102807

30 WHAT'S OUTSIDE A NAME?
1. Ang Lee
2. Tina Fey
3. Maya Lin
4. Tim Roth
5. Mae West
6. Ray Kroc
7. Meg Ryan
8. Ayn Rand
9. Ernie Els
10. Moss Hart
11. Juan Gris
12. Eva Perón
13. Tom Hulce
14. Babe Ruth
15. Anne Rice
16. Leon Uris
17. Eric Idle
18. Tori Amos
19. Alan King
20. Rita Dove
21. Spike Lee
22. Mel Blanc
23. Brian Eno
24. Dan Savage
25. Ivan Lendl
26. Tom Clancy
27. Ted Turner
28. Sam Mendes
29. Dan Rather
30. Matt Damon
31. Alan Moore
32. Lena Horne
33. Ted Hughes
34. Tony Blair
35. Gene Autry
36. Usain Bolt
37. Ella Raines
38. Jules Verne
39. Carl Reiner
40. Eli Manning
41. Jane Austen
42. Paris Hilton
43. Otis Redding
44. Tony Randall
45. Oliver Stone

32 TEAMWORK
1. Celtics, Bruins; Boston
2. Dolphins, Heat; Miami
3. Bears, White Sox; Chicago
4. Raiders, Athletics; Oakland
5. Dodgers, Clippers; Los Angeles
6. Lions, Tigers; Detroit
7. Yankees, Islanders; New York
8. Rams, Cardinals; St. Louis
9. Ravens, Orioles; Baltimore
10. Redskins, Capitals; Washington
11. Steelers, Pirates; Pittsburgh
12. Suns, Coyotes; Phoenix
13. Cowboys, Stars; Dallas
14. Rangers, Liberty; New York
15. Phillies, Flyers; Philadelphia
16. Falcons, Hawks; Atlanta
17. Brewers, Bucks; Milwaukee
18. Chiefs, Royals; Kansas City
19. Colts, Pacers; Indianapolis
20. Pistons, Red Wings; Detroit
21. Broncos, Nuggets; Denver
22. Bills, Sabres; Buffalo
23. Rockets, Astros; Houston

24. Seahawks, Mariners; Seattle
25. Chargers, Padres; San Diego
26. Bengals, Reds; Cincinnati
27. Nationals, Wizards; Washington
28. Raptors, Maple Leafs; Toronto
29. Indians, Cavaliers; Cleveland
30. Buccaneers, Lightning; Tampa Bay
31. Braves, Thrashers; Atlanta
32. Saints, Hornets; New Orleans
33. Spurs, Silver Stars; San Antonio
34. Canadiens, Impact; Montreal
35. Flames, Stampeders; Calgary
36. Blue Jackets, Crew; Columbus
37. Blue Jays, Argonauts
38. Sounders FC, Storm; Seattle

34 JIGSAW SQUARES 3

36 ENTERTAINMENT OPTIONS

1. *Home Alone*
2. *Howards End*
3. *[The] Big Sleep*
4. "Tainted Love"
5. *Dick Tracy*
6. *Native Son*
7. *Breaking Bad*
8. *Grey Gardens*
9. *Naked Lunch*
10. *Starship Troopers*
11. *Chicago Hope*
12. *Perry Mason*
13. "Lovely Rita"
14. *[The] Brady Brides*
15. *Lou Grant*
16. *[The] Iceman Cometh*
17. *[The] Scarlet Letter*
18. *Project Runway*
19. *Pale Fire*
20. "Manic Monday"
21. *[The] Lovely Bones*
22. *[The] Wedding Singer*
23. *Missile Command*
24. *Golden Boy*
25. *[The] West Wing*
26. *[The] French Chef*
27. *American Pie*
28. *[A] Simple Plan*
29. "[The] Hollow Men"

30. *Ender's Game*
31. *China Beach*
32. *Billy Madison*
33. *Silent Spring*
34. *Main Street*
35. "Paper Planes"
36. *[The] Ipcress File*
37. *Animal Farm*
38. *Imperial Bedroom*
39. *[The] Hurt Locker*
40. *Gorky Park*
41. *[The] Devil's Dictionary*
42. "Gold Digger"
43. *[The] Wonder Years*
44. Pole Position
45. *[A] Thousand Acres*
46. *Solitary Man*
47. *[The] Sheltering Sky*
48. "Bad Romance"
49. *Spirited Away*
50. "Aloha Oe"

38 DROPQUOTE/FLOATQUOTE

1. I don't need you to remind me of my age: I have a bladder to do that for me.
2. I believe in luck: how else can you explain the success of those you dislike?

39 BLANKING OUT 3

1. Cheeses
BEDFRAME (Edam)
GROUND BALL (Gouda)
FESTIVAL (feta)
EMBROIDER (Brie)
HEAVY ARTILLERY (Havarti)
SWIFTNESS (Swiss)
SCHOOLBOY (Colby)
UNSPORTSMANLIKE CONDUCT
   (Port-Salut)

2. Dog breeds
PAKISTAN (Akita)
SPANISH OMELET (spaniel)
HOTEL PROPRIETOR (terrier)
COMPOUND INTEREST (pointer)
BEDRAGGLED (beagle)
COLLAPSIBLE (collie)
BRONX CHEER (boxer)
HOSPITALIZE (spitz)
BROKE FRESH GROUND
   (keeshond)
SMALL INTESTINE (Maltese)
PARTS PER MILLION (papillon)
PECULIARITY (puli)

3. Types of car
ASCENDANT (sedan)
DECOUPAGE (coupe)
LEITMOTIF (limo)
BROADCASTER (roadster)
JAILKEEPER (jeep)
COMPLEX FRACTION (compact)

4. Crayola colors
CALENDAR YEAR (canary)
CHAMELEON (melon)
DANCE DANCE REVOLUTION
   (dandelion)
BURIAL MOUND (almond)
BELOW AVERAGE (beaver)
MODERN TIMES (denim)
SPILLED OVER (silver)
FINDING NEMO (indigo)
FACTORY WHISTLE (thistle)
MIDAFTERNOON (maroon)
MUSICAL HARMONY (salmon)
CLODHOPPER (copper)
RICE KRISPIES (cerise)
COLLECTIVE AGREEMENT (olive
   green)
SKEPTICAL (sepia)

40 CUT IT OUT

1. huge hug
2. damp amp
3. buoy boy
4. short shot
5. brush Bush
6. clean clan
7. swami swam
8. small mall
9. teeny teen
10. limbo limb
11. early earl
12. spare spar
13. brass bras
14. rapid raid
15. sharp harp
16. Garbo garb
17. camel came
18. pilot plot
19. sitar star
20. bellow below
21. burgle bugle
22. morose moose
23. golfer gofer
24. sturdy study
25. bluish blush
26. cosmic comic
27. guests guess
28. hoarse horse
29. launch lunch
30. resign reign
31. hanger anger
32. mainly manly
33. deduce deuce
34. mister miser
35. claims clams
36. pauper paper
37. oompah oomph
38. cartoon carton
39. pursues purses
40. spriest priest
41. Barbie's babies
42. careful carful
43. rooster roster
44. applies apples
45. theater heater
46. discuss discus
47. coroner corner
48. thirsty thirty
49. intuits Inuits
50. auction action
51. carless caress
52. pleasant peasant
53. puddling pudding
54. choosier Hoosier
55. Montague montage
56. catchall catcall
57. needless needles
58. Penzance penance
59. startling starling
60. addictive additive
61. hermitage heritage
62. impalement implement
63. altercation alteration

42 DOUBLE PLAY

1. COIN COLLECTOR
2. JANET JACKSON
3. CANDID CAMERA
4. POLE POSITION
5. DIRE DISTRESS
6. PAJAMA PARTY
7. BOOGIE BOARD
8. GOLDEN GOOSE
9. FRIZ FRELENG
10. SEVENTH SEAL
11. ACUTE ACCENT
12. SHORT SHRIFT
13. CAB CALLOWAY
14. HOLD HOSTAGE
15. MIRACLE MILE
16. GREEN GRAPES
17. MODEST MOUSE
18. STAND STILL
19. ROUND ROBIN
20. FLASH FLOOD
21. RACHAEL RAY
22. MASS MARKET
23. SEA SERPENT
24. GIBSON GIRL
25. SHELL SHOCK
26. MAID MARIAN
27. CATTLE CALL
28. LOCH LOMOND
29. WHITE WHALE
30. PITCH PIPE
31. TUMMY TUCK
32. BILL BIXBY
33. LAST LAUGH
34. NEURAL NET
35. ROMAN ROAD
36. TEXAS TECH
37. JUDGE JUDY
38. BEER BELLY
39. VOICE VOTE
40. FACE FACTS
41. CALICO CAT
42. FRENCH FRY
43. WASP WAIST
44. INDIA INK
45. GAS GAUGE
46. TALL TALE
47. POLO PONY
48. LAVA LAMP
49. ALAN ALDA
50. LOST LOVE
51. MACHO MAN
52. CABLE CAR
53. PET PEEVE
54. KEN KESEY
55. LIFE LIST
56. SABER SAW
57. LOS LOBOS
58. BIG BIRD
59. HARD HAT
60. REX REED
61. WAGE WAR
62. RAT RACE
63. MAD MAX
64. ROB ROY

44 INTERNAL AFFAIRS 2

1.
SI(DETRA)CK = D
T(ROMB)ONE = R
O(STEOP)ATH = O
S(EASH)ELL = S
PA(CESE)TTER = S
B(RATW)URST = W
PE(RIPHER)AL = H
LEG(ITIM)ACY = I
PER(MANEN)T = N
P(REDEST)INED = E
Bonus: DROSS WHINE =
DRO(WSINE)SS

2.
PR(OLIFER)ATE = F
S(LEEP)WEAR = L
COM(PROMIS)E = I
POR(CUPIN)E = N
STAL(AGMIT)E = G
AC(CLAMA)TION = A
P(ROSPER)ITY = S
HE(SITAT)ED = T
COM(MENCE)MENT = E
FAT(HERLINES)S = R
Bonus: FLING ASTER =
FL(ATTER)ING

45 CAMOUFLAGE
1. PING-PONG
2. RUN WILD
3. TAP DANCE
4. TOP GUN
5. TIME LAG
6. PETER PAN
7. TOLL CALL
8. KEY LIME
9. WIND CHIME
10. FREE AGENT
11. ANGEL HAIR
12. RUSH ORDER
13. EXIT VISA
14. DOWN UNDER
15. ONCE-OVER
16. CHOP SHOP
17. AUTO RACE
18. RED PANDA
19. EVIL TWIN
20. SUN HAT
21. FLAME WAR
22. RUMP ROAST
23. PINE TREE
24. ROB ROY
25. LOW-TECH
26. BONE CHINA
27. ANTIC MUSE
28. ART DECO
29. LOCAL HERO
30. TWO CENTS

46 STATE DEPARTMENT
1-ii. SQUID, SQUALID (Alabama)
2-t. BEAM IN, BENJAMIN (New Jersey)
3-xx. FILET, FILM SET (Mississippi)
4-aa. CHEER, CHEWIER (Wisconsin)
5-x. BRONC, BRONCHI (Hawaii)
6-b. PINTO, PIMENTO (Maine)
7-ll. COALESCE, CONVALESCE (Nevada)
8-y. INTER, INKSTER (Kansas)
9-bb. SINE, SINEWY (Wyoming)
10-nn. ENS, V-TENS (Vermont)
11-v. COEN, CON MEN (New Mexico)
12-ff. CHINO, CHINOOK (Oklahoma)
13-a. DENOUEMENT, DENOUNCEMENT (North Carolina)
14-h. MANNA, MANN ACT (Connecticut)
15-g. BOOMIE, BONHOMIE (New Hampshire)
16-ww. UNDRESS, LAUNDRESS (Louisiana)
17-uu. BRAHMS, BRAHMINS (Indiana)

18-l. VERMOUTH, RIVER MOUTH (Rhode Island)

19-vv. SLIGHT, SKYLIGHT (Kentucky)

20-d. PAWN, P.M. DAWN (Maryland)

21-c. ACCENT, ACCIDENT (Idaho)

22-gg. DRY ALE, DRYSDALE (South Dakota)

23-s. NEATER, MANEATER (Massachusetts)

24-w. MACHO, MACH ONE (Nebraska)

25-z. FOREST, FORECAST (California)

26-kk. DOCILE, DOMICILE (Michigan)

27-p. FARSI, FAR SIDE (Delaware)

28-r. SOLE, SOLEMN (Minnesota)

29-jj. WALLOWER, WALLFLOWER (Florida)

30-o. PRONE, PROPANE (Pennsylvania)

31-f. IN THE RED, INGATHERED (Georgia)

32-tt. HARDING, HAZARDING (Arizona)

33-k. EPSON, EPSILON (Illinois)

34-q. STANZA, COSTANZA (Colorado)

35-oo. CERES, COHERES (Ohio)

36-hh. DELISH, DEMOLISH (Missouri)

37-i. CROON, CROUTON (Utah)

38-e. AVENGER, SCAVENGER (South Carolina)

39-n. AMBLE, AMIABLE (Iowa)

40-cc. SHIITE, SHIITAKE (Alaska)

41-m. HINES, WAHINES (Washington)

42-u. SAI, SAW VI (West Virginia)

43-ee. ABUSES, MTA BUSES (Montana)

44-rr. PLANE, PLANET X (Texas)

45-mm. MOOSE, VAMOOSE (Virginia)

46-qq. PANAMA, PANORAMA (Oregon)

47-pp. AMORE, ANYMORE (New York)

48-j. THEBES, THE BENDS (North Dakota)

49-dd. SICK, ST. NICK (Tennessee)

50-ss. UNCLE, UNCLEAR (Arkansas)

50 TOO MANY QUOTES

1. BABBLE ("That'll do, pig. That'll do"; James Cromwell, *Babe* + "Frankly, my dear, I don't give a damn"; **Clark Gable**, *Gone With the Wind*)

2. JERKINS ("You had me at 'hello'"; Renée Zellweger, *Jerry Maguire*; "A census taker once tried to test me. I ate his liver with some fava beans and a nice chianti"; **Anthony Hopkins**, *The Silence of the Lambs*)

3. CADAVER ("Cinderella story. Outta nowhere. A former greenskeeper, now, about to become the Masters champion. It looks like a mirac... It's in the hole! It's in the hole! It's in the hole!"; Bill Murray, *Caddyshack* + "This is Ripley, last survivor of The Nostromo, signing off"; **Sigourney Weaver**, *Alien*)

4. FIGMENT ("You do not talk about Fight Club"; Brad Pitt, *Fight Club* + "I see dead people"; **Haley Joel Osment**, *The Sixth Sense*)

5. GLORIOUS ("All right, Mr. DeMille, I'm ready for my close-up"; **Gloria Swanson**, *Sunset Blvd.* + "I am a golden god!"; Billy Crudup, *Almost Famous*)

6. INGRATE ("Kiss me. Kiss me as if it were the last time"; **Ingrid Bergman**, *Casablanca* + "Mrs. Robinson, you're trying to seduce me. Aren't you?"; Dustin Hoffman, ***The Graduate***)

7. KEISTER ("Open the pod bay doors, HAL"; **Keir Dullea**, *2001: A Space Odyssey* + "The pellet with the poison's in the vessel with the pestle"; Danny Kaye, ***The Court Jester***)

8. TONALLY ("I'm Spartacus!"; **Tony Curtis**, *Spartacus* + "I'll have what she's having"; Estelle Reiner, ***When Harry Met Sally***)

9. SUPINE ("Kneel before Zod!"; Terence Stamp, ***Superman II*** + "Good night, you princes of Maine, you kings of New England"; **Michael Caine**, *The Cider House Rules*)

10. DENTURE ("Once the bus goes 50 miles an hour, the bomb is armed. If it drops below 50, it blows up. What do you do? What do you do?"; **Dennis Hopper**, *Speed* + "I know you are, but what am I?"; Paul Reubens, ***Pee-Wee's Big Adventure***)

11. CHARADE ("Soylent green is people!"; **Charlton Heston**, *Soylent Green* + "I like them French fried potaters"; Billy Bob Thornton, ***Sling Blade***)

12. MARCHERS ("Stella! Hey, Stella!"; **Marlon Brando**, *A Streetcar Named Desire* + "They're here already! You're next! You're next!"; Kevin McCarthy, ***Invasion of the Body Snatchers***)

13. TERRACE ("He's not the messiah, he's a very naughty boy"; **Terry Jones**, *Monty Python's Life of Brian* + "Say hello to my little friend!"; Al Pacino, ***Scarface***)

14. FARAWAY ("You betcha!"; Frances McDormand, ***Fargo*** + "She's my sister! She's my daughter!"; **Faye Dunaway**, *Chinatown*)

15. BRANCH ("They may take away our lives, but they'll never take our freedom!"; Mel Gibson, ***Braveheart*** + "I'm as mad as hell, and I'm not going to take this anymore!"; **Peter Finch**, *Network*)

16. PHILANDER ("Why are frogs falling from the sky?"; **Philip Seymour Hoffman**, *Magnolia* + "I feel like I'm taking crazy pills"; Will Ferrell, ***Zoolander***)

17. BETTERMENT ("Fasten your seatbelts. It's going to be a bumpy night"; **Bette Davis**, *All About Eve* + "I'd rather stick needles in my eyes"; Jack Nicholson, ***Terms of Endearment***)

18. BODKIN ("You aren't too bright. I like that in a man"; Kathleen Turner, ***Body Heat*** + "Hello. My name is Inigo Montoya. You killed my father. Prepare to die!"; **Mandy Patinkin**, *The Princess Bride*)

19. CHIEFLY ("There ain't no sanity clause!"; **Chico Marx**, *A Night at the Opera* + "Be afraid. Be very afraid"; Geena Davis, ***The Fly***)

20. EDAMAME ("This is crazy. I finally meet my childhood hero and he's trying to kill us. What a joke"; **Ed Asner**, *Up*; "Life is a banquet, and most poor suckers are starving to death!"; Rosalind Russell, ***Auntie Mame***)

21. JUNIPER ("Nah, I mean, I'm already pregnant, so what other kind of shenanigans could I get into?"; Ellen Page, ***Juno*** + "I have come here to chew bubble gum and kick ass, and I'm all out of bubble gum"; **Roddy Piper**, *They Live*)

22. CATCALL ("Let me see if I've got this straight: in order to be grounded, I've got to be crazy and I must be crazy to keep flying. But if I ask to be grounded, that means I'm not crazy any more and I have to keep flying"; Alan Arkin, ***Catch-22*** + "I love the smell of napalm in the morning"; **Robert Duvall**, *Apocalypse Now*)

23. MANTEL ("I think people should mate for life, like pigeons or Catholics"; Woody Allen, ***Manhattan*** + "That's exactly why we want to produce this play. To show the world the true Hitler, the Hitler you loved, the Hitler you knew, the Hitler with a song in his heart"; **Zero Mostel**, *The Producers*)

24. COLINEAR ("In this grave hour, perhaps the most fateful in history, I send to every household of my peoples, both at home and overseas, this message, spoken with the same depth of feeling for each one of you as if I were able to cross your threshold and speak to you myself"; **Colin Firth**, *The King's Speech* + "Come out, come out, wherever you are!"; Robert De Niro, ***Cape Fear***)

52 HALF AND HALF
1-t. BANISH, PUNDIT
2-b. BISQUE, BARHOP
3-m. BOTTLE, LITANY
4-j. BURDEN, GARGLE
5-s. CONFAB, PREFER
6-c. CRADLE, CANYON
7-u. DOCENT, RECTOR
8-i. EFFORT, EXPECT
9-d. FELINE, CANONS
10-w. FLOWER, SHOCKS
11-l. FOURTH, HEALER
12-y. GRIPPE, STENCH
13-f. GUIDED, CORNEA
14-v. HUMMED, SHAMUS
15-z. MISTER, WINERY
16-h. NATURE, ENDIVE
17-q. ORIOLE, PARENT
18-r. PARKAS, POLISH
19-e. PROPEL, COMFIT
20-k. RANGES, GAUCHO
21-n. RESIGN, MALTED
22-p. SENTRY, PALATE
23-x. SQUASH, SPLINT
24-o. TRAVEL, MARSHY
25-g. TREMOR, ENABLE
26-a. VALLEY, BARIUM

53 BLANKING OUT 4
1. Spices
COUNT ME IN (cumin)
PIED PIPER (pepper)
SCHMALTZ (salt)
SLANT RHYME (thyme)
DISAGREE (sage)
BASILISK (basil)
NORWEGIAN WOOD (oregano)
CARRIED AWAY (caraway)
DIMLY LIT (dill)
VICTORIA AND ALBERT
  (coriander)
GRANDIOSE (anise)
SELF-AFFIRMATION (saffron)
FALLEN ANGEL (fennel)
PLEASUREFUL (laurel)
MIDPOINT (mint)
GOLDFINGER (ginger)
PAULINA PORIZKOVA (paprika)
WASTEPAPER BIN (wasabi)
MACABRE (mace)
RITCHIE VALENS (chives)
GERMAN REPUBLIC (garlic)
SALVATION ARMY (savory)
TURKISH-AMERICAN (turmeric)

2. Comic strips
POLYGON ("Pogo")
SUPERANNUATES ("Peanuts")
LOCALLY EUCLIDEAN SPACE
  ("Cul-de-Sac")
ZEITGEIST ("Zits")
LITHUANIAN ("Luann")
ENTRANCEWAY ("Nancy")
MULTITASK ("Mutts")
SECURITY RISK ("Curtis")
SCHMOOZE ("Shoe")
DIAMOND LIL ("Dondi")
SCROLL LOCK ("Crock")
MOHAMMEDAN ("Momma")
COUNTERBALANCED ("Outland")
MIRA SORVINO ("Marvin")

3. Gambling games
BACCALAUREATE (baccarat)
CRABAPPLES (craps)
FACTORY OUTLET STORE
  (roulette)
SLOW BUT SURE (slots)
PLAYING DOWN (pai gow)
FANTASYLAND (fan-tan)

54 CRYPTO-MINIS
1. THE TELL-TALE HEART
2. COCA-COLA CLASSIC
3. RUNNING GAG
4. CATCH-AS-CATCH CAN
5. BEANIE BABIES
6. TREADED WATER
7. BLUE-BLOODED
8. GEORGE ORWELL
9. COLLECT CALL
10. ROSES ARE RED
11. BYE BYE BIRDIE
12. TENNESSEE TITANS
13. GINGER BEER
14. ROSH HASHANAH
15. SASSAFRAS TEA
16. THOUGHT THROUGH
17. ANNA KARENINA
18. SESAME STREET
19. HAILE SELASSIE
20. NERVE CENTER
21. ASSISTANT LIBRARIAN
22. NO MAN IS AN ISLAND
23. SLEEPLESS IN SEATTLE
24. TAKES A CLOSE LOOK
25. AS SCARCE AS HEN'S TEETH
26. PHILADELPHIA PHILLIES
27. ANTARCTIC OCEAN
28. THIS TOO SHALL PASS
29. STANDS AT ATTENTION
30. THE SWEET HEREAFTER
31. QUINQUENNIALLY
32. CABLE ACCESS CHANNEL
33. RENAISSANCE MAN

34. PICTURE PERFECT
35. CLERICAL COLLARS
36. AFFAIR OF THE HEART
37. MICROPROCESSOR
38. GREEN GODDESS DRESSING
39. MARIE ANTOINETTE
40. TREATED TO DINNER
41. HIPPOCRATIC OATH
42. GENE RODDENBERRY
43. SEATING ASSIGNMENT
44. DAME EDNA EVERAGE
45. TINTINNABULATION

57 MIXED MESSAGES 3
1. Apart from the known and the unknown, what else is there?
2. I always invest in companies an idiot could run, because one day one will.
3. In order to be irreplaceable one must always be different.

58 CHARACTERS WITH CHARACTER
1. Peter Pan
2. Jane Eyre
3. Lois Lane
4. Emma Peel
5. Boba Fett
6. Sam Spade
7. Amy March
8. Rob Petrie
9. Bill Sikes
10. Axel Foley
11. Don Draper
12. Mace Windu
13. Roxie Hart
14. Tom Ripley
15. Lara Croft
16. Boo Radley
17. Nero Wolfe
18. Willy Wonka
19. Perry Mason
20. Ally McBeal
21. Opie Taylor
22. Darth Vader
23. Steve Urkel
24. Bruce Wayne
25. Dorian Gray
26. Hikaru Sulu
27. Big Brother
28. Bob Cratchit
29. Eddie Felson
30. Rhett Butler
31. Hedda Gabler
32. Harry Potter
33. Sal Paradise
34. Cosmo Kramer
35. Sally Bowles
36. Bagger Vance
37. Brainy Smurf
38. Gregor Samsa
39. Nora Charles
40. Ricky Ricardo
41. Dexter Morgan
42. Inigo Montoya
43. Maynard Krebs
44. Stuart Little
45. Napoleon Solo
46. Norma Desmond
47. Rainbow Brite
48. Barney Rubble
49. Marge Simpson
50. Oscar Madison
51. Austin Powers
52. Severus Snape
53. Frasier Crane
54. Veronica Mars
55. Lennie Briscoe
56. Blanche DuBois
57. Ignatius Reilly
58. Roseanne Conner
59. Carrie Bradshaw
60. Dorothea Brooke
61. Morticia Addams
62. Waylon Smithers
63. Edward Rochester

60 MISDIRECTION 2

1-Across: SPARE TIRE (six-pack)
10-Across: STARBOARD (port)
11-Across: ROBINSON CRUSOE (Friday)
14-Across: ST. GEORGE (drag on = dragon)
26-Across: PIANO (forte)
1-Down: WANE (wax)
3-Down: PREJUDICE (pride)
7-Down: GABBANA (*Dolce*)
12-Down: WATER WORKS (*Electric Company*)
15-Down: SCOOBY-DOO (shaggy)
16-Down: BRAND-NEW (second hand)
18-Down: SERVANT (master)
20-Down: DRACULA (bat)
21-Down: CREDIT (Cash)
23-Down: EXITS (entrances)

62 PUT IT BACK

1. fast feast
2. fair fakir
3. reel rebel
4. sage Saget
5. pert Perot
6. caper capper
7. gnome genome
8. party parity
9. dingy dinghy
10. inter Pinter
11. naive native
12. reuse refuse
13. irate pirate
14. ample sample
15. morel morsel
16. Camus campus
17. stale stable
18. whisk whisky
19. reedy remedy
20. limber climber
21. garish garnish
22. potent portent
23. curing cursing
24. benign Benigni
25. potion portion
26. shogun shotgun
27. covert convert
28. faulty faculty
29. sandal scandal
30. lazier glazier
31. bitter bittern
32. louses' lotuses
33. unties aunties
34. causes cayuses
35. garage garbage

117

36. outage outrage
37. galley gallery
38. assist bassist
39. trophy atrophy
40. ensure censure
41. Hanover hangover
42. slander Islander
43. risking frisking
44. flaming flamingo
45. antigun Antiguan
46. Pershing perishing
47. insulting insulating
48. rainstorm brainstorm

64 DROPQUOTE/FLOATQUOTE 2

1. I hate flowers. I paint them because they're cheaper than models and they don't move.
2. Diplomats are just as essential for starting a war as soldiers are for finishing it.

65 CENTRAL LOCATIONS

1. Berlin, Germany
2. Madrid, Spain
3. Lima, Peru

4. Amsterdam, Netherlands
5. Accra, Ghana
6. Belgrade, Serbia
7. Ankara, Turkey
8. Dublin, Ireland
9. Buenos Aires, Argentina
10. Copenhagen, Denmark
11. Maseru, Lesotho
12. Tallinn, Estonia
13. Montevideo, Uruguay
14. Bucharest, Romania
15. Kathmandu, Nepal
16. Tunis, Tunisia
17. Cairo, Egypt
18. Manila, Philippines
19. Nairobi, Kenya
20. Riga, Latvia
21. Damascus, Syria
22. Sucre, Bolivia
23. Monrovia, Liberia
24. Quito, Ecuador
25. San Salvador, El Salvador
26. Muscat, Oman
27. Santo Domingo, Dominican Republic
28. Singapore, Singapore
29. Helsinki, Finland

66 JIGSAW SQUARES 4

68 ENTERTAINMENT OPTIONS 2

1. "Three Blind Mice"
2. "Whole Lotta Love"
3. *Good Will Hunting*
4. *[The] Cider House Rules*
5. "When Doves Cry"
6. *Dances With Wolves*
7. *[A] Hard Day's Night*
8. *Saving Private Ryan*
9. "Song Sung Blue"
10. *Thelma and Louise*
11. "Auld Lang Syne"
12. *West Side Story*
13. "[The] Road Not Taken"
14. "Secret Agent Man"
15. *[The] Kitchen God's Wife*
16. "Please Please Me"
17. *Father Knows Best*
18. "What's Going On?"
19. *Six Feet Under*
20. *Hill Street Blues*
21. "Big Yellow Taxi"
22. *Brave New World*
23. *Gas Food Lodging*
24. *East of Eden*
25. "Theme From *Shaft*"
26. *Cool Hand Luke*
27. Super Mario Bros.
28. *Freaks and Geeks*
29. *One Trick Pony*
30. *[The] Sun Also Rises*
31. "Hot Cross Buns"
32. *Women in Love*
33. *[The] Palm Beach Story*
34. "I'll Cry Instead"
35. *Eyes Wide Shut*
36. "Seven Nation Army"
37. *Black Hawk Down*
38. *Coal Miner's Daughter*
39. *[The] Lavender Hill Mob*
40. "Miss Otis Regrets"
41. *Destry Rides Again*
42. *Shall We Dance?*
43. *Barney and Friends*
44. "Oye Como Va"
45. Metal Gear Solid

46. *Last Tango in Paris*
47. *Much Ado About Nothing*
48. *When Harry Met Sally*
49. *Look Back in Anger*
50. *Peggy Sue Got Married*
51. "My Best Friend's Girl"
52. "Won't Get Fooled Again"
53. *There Will Be Blood*
54. *Some Like It Hot*
55. *Seems Like Old Times*
56. *What's Eating Gilbert Grape*
57. "Death Be Not Proud"
58. *From Here to Eternity*

70 MIX-INS

1. TRIPE + MANLY = PERMIT, PIRATE, PINTER, TRIPLE, PYRITE
2. PLANET + GORY = PANT LEG, POLENTA, PLANTER, PENALTY
3. LINGER + TEMPOS = RINGLET, REELING, GREMLIN, PRINGLE, GONERIL, SERLING
4. MASTER + WHIRLED = WARMEST, HAMSTER, ARTEMIS, ARMREST, MR. SLATE, STEAMER, SMARTED
5. LEADEN + WRIT = NEW DEAL, LEANDER, ADELINE, AL DENTE
6. CERTAIN + TOILS = INTERACT, CREATION, IN A TRICE, CLARINET, SCANTIER
7. STONE + KING RALPH = TOKENS, ON-SITE, SONNET, STENOG, TENSOR, ATONES, STOLEN, NO PETS, HONEST
8. RECAST + HOT LIPS = THE CARS, COASTER, SCATTER, SCARLET, RACIEST, SPECTRA, ACTRESS
9. SILKEN + VESTRY = KELVINS, EELSKIN, INKLESS, SILENT K, RELINKS, SKYLINE
10. STRIPE + CHISEL = TRICEPS, HIPSTER, TIPSIER, PERSIST, RESPITE, LETS RIP

11. RED GIANT + SHAME =
ART DESIGN, THREADING,
TRAGEDIAN, GREAT MIND,
DENIGRATE

73 INTERNAL AFFAIRS 3
1.
NA(RRAT)IVE = R
SQU(EAM)ISH = E
TE(LEMARK)ETER = L
P(OLY)ESTER = Y
MA(TRIMO)NY = O
MA(NEUVE)R = U
F(OOTS)ORE = T
SPE(ARMI)NT = I
DI(SHEVEL)ED = E
Bonus: RELY OUTIE =
R(OUTIN)ELY

2.
IN(TROV)ERT = V
NO(MINATE)D = A
WA(RRANT)Y = R
DE(MYST)IFY = Y
TI(METAB)LE = B
HAMM(ERL)OCK = L
IMP(RUDENT)LY = U
DI(VIDEN)D = N
S(UNBAT)HED = T
Bonus: VARY BLUNT =
V(OLUNT)ARY

74 STRIKE THREE
1. BEARDED LADY
2. FROZEN PIZZA
3. HEAD HONCHO
4. SUMMERTIME
5. FINAL OFFER
6. HORSE SENSE
7. IN MEMORIAM
8. IVAN PAVLOV
9. SATURNALIA
10. FISTICUFFS
11. WIDOW'S WALK
12. SONNY BONO
13. CHIHUAHUA
14. ARBITRARY
15. HIGH HOPES
16. COBWEBBED
17. TEST PILOT
18. AGGREGATE
19. CAT LITTER
20. KERFUFFLE
21. LEGAL PLEA
22. SLAP-HAPPY
23. HIT THE HAY
24. YAKETY-YAK
25. TWIST TIES
26. CIRCUS ACT
27. LUFTWAFFE
28. ANTITRUST
29. INANITIES
30. SOLIPSIST
31. ACCURACY
32. MAMA BEAR
33. PAPER CUP
34. CORRIDOR
35. DAY BY DAY
36. BABY BOOM
37. PETE ROSE
38. BILLFOLD
39. NINTENDO
40. SIGHT GAG
41. FOUL ODOR
42. RED ROVER
43. DC COMICS
44. FLOTILLA
45. ALIBI IKE
46. SUCCINCT
47. DIVIDEND
48. TERAWATT
49. CINNAMON
50. DOGGY BAG
51. SISYPHUS
52. HABAKKUK
53. BELL LABS
54. SCIROCCO
55. SYNONYMY
56. APT PUPIL
57. O SOLE MIO
58. GOOSE EGG
59. STILETTO

60. IN UNISON
61. MC HAMMER
62. USURIOUS
63. ALL TALK
64. LULLABY
65. IDI AMIN

76 MIXED MESSAGES 4

1. Several excuses are always less convincing than one.
2. Somehow or other I'll be famous, and if not famous, I'll be notorious.
3. Dinners are given mostly in the middle classes by way of revenge.

77 BAD PAIR DAY

1-aa. AS USUAL, BOBOLINK
2-y. ACTIVE VERB, ROB A BANK
3-m. ASININE, HONOLULU
4-b. BEAR ARMS, COCOON
5-bb. CANTATA, CUCUMBER
6-e. CONFRERE, BUDDY SYSTEM
7-g. CRISIS, CATATONIC
8-u. CREPE PAPER, PLUG-UGLY
9-l. DIETETIC, HAS A SHOT
10-k. DRAMAMINE, EUROPOP
11-o. ULULATE, JAGGED EDGE
12-s. FRENCH CHEF, ONENESS
13-a. GOOF OFF, ALMA MATER
14-c. IMBIBING, PAPAYA
15-f. KOBE BEEF, CHAKA KHAN
16-r. MEMENTO, L.A. LAKERS
17-j. LAZY EYE, ELI LILLY
18-d. LENINIST, BROUHAHA
19-z. MIMICRY, SLYLY
20-ee. MAPLE LEAF, VIRTUOSOS
21-q. MISO SOUP, MAUD ADAMS
22-p. MILLILITER, JUJUBES
23-i. PAS DE DEUX, ICICLE
24-t. PETTY TYRANT,
   OPEN-ENDED
25-dd. PETITION, YO-YO MA
26-v. SCI-FI FAN, PROTOTYPE
27-h. SORORITY, COLLEGE GRAD
28-x. STOWAWAY, REST STOP

29-cc. TASTE TEST, KOKOMO
30-ff. TAX-EXEMPT, VUVUZELA
31-w. THIS IS IT, RETRO ROCKET
32-n. TOPO GIGIO, HORSE SENSE

78 SKELETON THREES

1. stop, drop, roll
2. love, honor, obey
3. wine, women, song
4. Olga, Masha, Irina
5. bell, book, candle
6. Huey, Dewey, Louie
7. crust, mantle, core
8. lock, stock, barrel
9. ready, willing, able
10. faith, hope, charity
11. lion, witch, wardrobe
12. Tinker, Evers, Chance
13. lather, rinse, repeat
14. past, present, future
15. Patty, Maxene, Laverne
16. Alvin, Simon, Theodore
17. lights, camera, action
18. fold, spindle, mutilate

81 BLANKING OUT 5

1. Beatles songs
WINDOWSILL ("I Will")
URSA MINOR ("Rain")
PENNSYLVANIA AVENUE
   ("Penny Lane")
HEALTH SPA ("Help!")
TIME MACHINE ("I Me Mine")
GIBRALTAR ("Girl")
ELECTRONIC TUBE ("Let It Be")
THREW OVERBOARD ("The Word")
MONOCHROME DISPLAY
   ("No Reply")
KUWAITI ("Wait")
JUGGLING ACT ("Julia")
HYPERSENSITIZES ("Yes It Is")
BOBBY-SOXER ("Boys")
INDIGNITY ("Dig It")
MICROSURGERY ("Misery")
SPELUNKING ("Sun King")
THREATENED ("The End")

2. Horsemen of the Apocalypse
PRESIDENTIAL RESIDENCE
  (Pestilence)
WISEACRE (War)
FAMILY NAME (Famine)
DECATHLON (Death)

3. Muppets
REORGANIZE (Ernie)
BABE RUTH (Bert)
WORK PERMIT (Kermit)
STATE LOTTERY (Statler)
THE ALAMO (Elmo)
GROUND COVER (Grover)
NERO WOLFE (Rowlf)
BOILERMAKER (Beaker)
ANTIMALARIAL (Animal)
ZOMBIE (Zoe)
UNDER THE WEATHER (Dr. Teeth)
JAUNDICED (Janice)
ROY ORBISON (Robin)
MOTHER COUNTRY (The Count)
ZERO MOSTEL (Zoot)
NONSECULAR (Oscar)
GORGONZOLA (Gonzo)

4. Flowers
AUDACIOUSLY (daisy)
IMPRISON (iris)
GROOMSMEN (rose)
PASS THE BAR (aster)
POSTER CHILD (orchid)
CROSSCUT SAW (crocus)
ELI WALLACH (lilac)

82 WHAT'S THE CONNECTION?
1. stick figure
2. paper tiger
3. full Monty
4. Joe Cocker
5. tunnel vision
6. Puff Daddy
7. cover letter
8. *Space Jam*
9. village idiot
10. butterfly
11. cable box
12. buzz cut
13. curtain call
14. tape deck
15. second hand
16. time travel
17. distance running
18. Julius Caesar
19. spoonbread
20. place setting
21. squash court
22. rangefinders
23. Cookie Monster
24. party pooper
25. sticker shock
26. action hero
27. sky-high
28. acid rain
29. soda fountain
30. bargain bin
31. machine gun
32. blind date
33. pepper-upper
34. hold everything
35. keg stand
36. Death Star
37. ball bearing
38. shot glass
39. drumbeat
40. stop short
41. mushroom cloud
42. comfort zone
43. Arcade Fire
44. jingle bell
45. ground round
46. pocket money
47. Klein bottle
48. felt-tip
49. box turtle
50. English Channel

84 MISDIRECTION 3

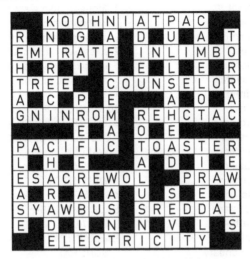

1-Across: CAPTAIN HOOK
(Peter Pan)
14-Across: MORNING (evening)
15-Across: CATCHER (pitcher)
21-Across: LOWERCASE (capital)
23-Across: WARP (woof)
25-Across: SUBWAYS (Els)
26-Across: LADDERS (snakes)
1-Down: ICE RINK (pool)
2-Down: IAGO (Othello)
3-Down: CAME CLEAN (lied)
7-Down: GATHER (scatter)
8-Down: CARROT (stick)
15-Down: INSULATOR (conductor)
20-Down: SLOWER (faster)
24-Down: IVES (currier)

86 SMALL CHANGE

1. huge luge
2. faux flux
3. abode above
4. decry decay
5. vague *Vogue*
6. adore adobe
7. Mafia mania
8. terse verse
9. wordy worry
10. lined linen
11. taboo Naboo
12. spook spoof
13. tries Aries
14. other otter
15. toxic topic
16. forgo Fargo
17. beats beaus
18. squid squib
19. camel cameo
20. scale scalp
21. nuked naked
22. chorus chords
23. decent docent
24. gander gender
25. ballet mallet
26. avoids ovoids
27. rocket racket
28. boring boxing
29. polite police
30. wintry winery
31. simple wimple
32. gauche gaucho
33. milder mildew
34. unwind upwind
35. sodium podium
36. "blecch, bleach"
37. yonder wonder
38. barber barter

39. kosher mosher
40. genial denial
41. divine diving
42. hermit permit
43. driest priest
44. hominy homily
45. bought nought
46. Carter career
47. parish pariah
48. Reuters routers
49. rustier rustler
50. hideous hideout
51. Palance balance
52. certain curtain
53. detects defects
54. hostage postage
55. lathers bathers
56. refutes refuges
57. Mandela mandala
58. chaster chapter
59. impress empress
60. massive missive
61. brutish British
62. noshing nothing
63. oration ovation
64. testify testily
65. profess prowess
66. sweeter sweater
67. patrols patrons
68. towards cowards
69. viscount discount
70. quitting quilting
71. frostier frontier
72. prisoner poisoner
73. appeared appeased
74. previous precious
75. stealing sterling
76. Nobelist novelist
77. nineties niceties
78. dwindling swindling
79. encourage entourage
80. channeling changeling
81. stationary stationery

89 DROPQUOTE/FLOATQUOTE 3

1. Money is like a sixth sense without which you cannot make a complete use of the other five.
2. It is always the best policy to tell the truth, unless, of course, you are an exceptionally good liar.

90 SOUND OFF

ABALONE (2-b, ASH + BOLOGNA)
AEROSOL (20-pp, HEIRESS + WALL)
ANTIQUATED (1-qq, ANTICS + WEIGHTED)
ASPHALT (3-o, ASK + FAULT)
BACCHANAL (5-e, BASH + CANAL)
BARRACUDA (4-d, BARRACK + BUDDHA)
BATTALION (6-s, BEAU + ITALIAN)
BELEAGUER (7-m, BELOW + EAGER)
BICYCLE (9-gg, BITE + SICKLE)
BISCOTTI (8-w, BISQUE + KNOTTY)
BULWARK (10-ff, BULL + QUARK)
CATALYST (11-aa, CATTLE + MIST)
CHAMPAGNE (38-dd, SHAM + PAINT)
CHARTREUSE (39-nn, SHARP + TRUCE)
COQUETTE (12-t, COKE + JET)
CORIANDER (13-z, CORE + MEANDER)
DEPRESSANT (15-k, DIP + CRESCENT)
DISTRICT (16-mm, DISK + TRICKED)
EQUINOX (17-v, EQUAL + KNOCKS)
GOSSAMER (19-bb, GOSSIP + MYRRH)
INTERLUDE (45-y, WINTER + LEWD)

LACKLUSTER (22-h, LAMB + CLUSTER)

LAGNIAPPE (33-ss, PLAN + YAP)

LICORICE (23-rr, LIQUOR + WISH)

MANNEQUIN (24-hh, MANNA + SKIN)

MARMALADE (25-x, MARMOT + LAID)

MELANCHOLY (26-i, MELANIE + COLLIE)

MISTREAT (27-jj, MIFF + STREET)

NOCTURNAL (21-u, KNOCKED + JOURNAL)

OPAQUE (41-a, TAUPE + ACHE)

PARACHUTE (29-c, PARISH + BOOT)

PARADISE (30-r, PARODY + ICE)

PERSNICKETY (35-cc, PURSE + NICOTINE)

PHALANX (18-ll, FAIL + THANKS)

PICARESQUE (31-l, PICKER + DESK)

PLAYGROUND (32-q, PLAGUE + FROWNED)

POPPYCOCK (40-ee, SPA + PEACOCK)

PROOFREAD (34-p, PRUNE + FREED)

SACCHARINE (36-j, SASH + CORINNE)

SINECURE (14-n, CYNIC + EURO)

SURVEILLANCE (37-oo, SERB + VALENCE)

TRIPTYCH (42-g, TRIPPED + CHICK)

TROUSSEAU (43-ii, TRUE + SOAP)

UNDAINTY (28-kk, MUNDANE + TEA)

WARFARE (47-f, WHARF + CHAIR)

92 JIGSAW SQUARES 5

94 I'VE GOT SOME LITTLE LISTS

1. Each word can have its first phoneme moved elsewhere to make a new word.

    THREE (wreath)
    FOREIGN (orphan)
    TENOR (enter)
    STRAY (trace)
    STRICTER (trickster)
d. DRIBBLE (ribald)

2. Each word can follow the name of a U.S. president in a phrase.

    (Ford) ESCORT
    (Lincoln) LOGS
    (Bush) LEAGUE
    (Hoover) VACUUM
    (Pierce) ARROW
f. (Cleveland) HEIGHTS

3. These are all words which are pluralized without adding "S."

    CHILD (children)
    GOOSE (geese)
    ADDENDUM (addenda)
    TOOTH (teeth)
    CRISIS (crises)
c. CRITERION (criteria)

4. Each word is a unit of measurement whose final letter has been replaced with a word.

    AMPERSAND (ampere + sand)
    MILLINER (mile + liner)
    GALLOPING (gallon + ping)
    PINAFORE (pint + afore)
    YARBOROUGH (yard + borough)
m. THEREON (therm + eon)

5. Each word, by deleting a letter and reversing what remains, spells a new word.

    AMTRAK (karma)
    DELILAH (hailed)
    REVISION (noisier)
    LLAMAS (small)
    ROMAINE (enamor)
    RESEAL (laser)
    STRAPPED (departs)
    GENIUS (suing)
e. EMERGED (degree)

6. Each word can have a color name deleted to leave a new word.

    STEALING (teal, sing)
    BOREDOM (red, boom)
    ALIMENT (lime, ant)
    SLUMBERED (umber, sled)
    BOTANY (tan, boy)
    TRUSTEE (rust, tee)
    ABASHED (ash, abed)
b. CLAMBERING (amber, cling)

7. Each word contains two consecutive letters that lie two positions apart in the alphabet (i.e., A and C, B and D, etc.) Replacing that pair of letters with the letter that comes between them produces a new word.

    COMMENCE (commend)
    DEMOTED (dented)
    LAWYER (laxer)
    CENSUS (cents)
    TREACLE (treble)
    EGOIST (foist)
l. SANDFLY (sanely)

8. Each word contains a series of four consecutive Roman numerals (and no others elsewhere).

    BOLLIX (LLIX)
    ELIMINATE (LIMI)
    ADVIL (DVIL)
    MIDDAY (MIDD)
    SERVICING (VICI)
i. PEMMICAN (MMIC)

9. All the letters but one in each word are in alphabetical order.

    GHOSTLY (L out of order)
    AILMENT (E out of order)

126

BEEFIEST (final E out of order)
CLUMSY (U out of order)
ACCIDENT (I out of order)
TAILORS (T out of order)
DEFIANT (A out of order)
BELLHOPS (H out of order)
a. ACHILLES (E out of order)

10. Each word or phrase corresponds to a dessert, ignoring the vowels in each one. That is, the consonants in ICE PICK (CPCK) are the same as the consonants in CUPCAKE (CPCK again).
ICE PICK (cupcake)
TORI AMOS (tiramisu)
PEPSI-COLA (popsicle)
ENPLANE (Napoleon)
EMBERS (ambrosia)
TOPIC (tapioca)
GUILT (gelato)
FELON (flan)
CHIRRUP (cherry pie)
j. PROFIT (parfait)

11. Each word, repeated one or more times, becomes a song title.
"CHERRY Cherry," Neil Diamond
"REBEL Rebel," David Bowie
"SAY Say Say," Paul McCartney and Michael Jackson
"YUMMY Yummy Yummy," Ohio Express
"PERHAPS, Perhaps, Perhaps," Doris Day
"SUGAR Sugar," the Archies
"MONDAY, Monday," the Mamas and the Papas
k. "RUSH Rush," Paula Abdul

12. Each word can have a letter deleted to make a word with one more syllable than the original word.
CORNMEAL (corneal)
FUGUE (fugu)

DRAGGED (ragged)
BEAUTIFY (beatify)
MOUSE (moue)
GLACIER (lacier)
RATION (ratio)
FINANCE (fiance)
GREENGAGE (reengage)
g. MOPPED (moped)

13. Each item on the list contains a Greek letter spelled backward.
DATEBOOK (beta or eta)
MIKE RATLEDGE (delta)
STAGE MOTHER (omega)
WHISPER (psi)
SQUAT (tau)
NIELS BOHR (rho)
h. PATOIS (iota)

96 CELEBRITY DOINGS
1. BEACONS
2. EARPHONES
3. SAMPANS
4. AXLED
5. CARAPACES
6. REDRAFTED
7. DIVERSIFIED
8. COOPERATE
9. GENERATED
10. MASTIFFS
11. ANIMATES
12. PATRIOTS
13. LINGOES
14. MARTINIS
15. CURTAILED
16. MAXIMS
17. LEADOFFS
18. HALLOWS
19. FORAGES
20. BRAMBLED
21. SCALAWAGS
22. BRANDISHED
23. PANCREASES
24. UPRAISES
25. LEND-LEASES

97 INTERNAL AFFAIRS 4

1.
LA(MBCHO)P = B
MI(SCREA)NT = A
TO(LLBO)OTH = L
MA(LARKE)Y = K
F(REEB)OOTING = B
DO(ORBE)LL = E
STRA(TEG)Y = T
PA(RAFF)IN = A
Bonus: BALK BETA = BA(BYTA)LK

2.
C(ARPENT)RY = P
W(ASTEL)AND = L
COL(ORATUR)A = U
DE(TRIMENT)AL = M
PAL(PITAT)E = T

F(ORETEL)LING = O
PE(NTAG)ON = N
INF(IELD)ER = I
AN(TARC)TIC = C
Bonus: PLUM TONIC =
PLU(TONIU)M

3.
POI(GNA)NT = A
BA(NKRO)LL = K
PE(STILEN)T = I
PLEA(SAN)T = N
CL(INGST)ONE = S
P(ROPEL)LED = L
P(ATERN)OSTER = A
PA(THOGE)N = G
Bonus: AKIN SLAG =
SLA(CKIN)G

98 THEM'S FIGHTING WORDS

8. SNOW/SNOB
9. HOARSE/HEARSE
10. SHELL/SHALL
11. TAKEI/TAKER
12. SIMPLE/SIMILE
13. WAVERED/
    WATERED

Altered words
(columns):
1. FLOSSED/
   GLOSSED
2. RECOMBING/
   RECOMBINE
3. ALLOW/ALLOT
4. PRAISE/BRAISE
5. ICON/IRON
6. REVEL/RAVEL
7. BRAND/BRAID
8. HITS/NITS
9. CHATTEL/CHATTED
10. SHLUB/SHRUB
11. DOUBLE/DOABLE
12. WANT/WAIT
13. SEEDLING/
    NEEDLING

From left to right, the circled letters read GET BRAIN DRAIN. From top to bottom, they read GRIN AND BEAR IT.

Altered words (rows):
1. ORATING/GRATING
2. LE PEW/LEPER
3. RAISON/RAISIN
4. ENROL/ENRON
5. SLIT/ALIT
6. DEAR/DEAN
7. BOGIE/DOGIE